WILL TO WIN

WILL TO WIN

New Zealand netball greats on team culture and leadership

LANA MCCARTHY, ANDY MARTIN
AND GEOFF WATSON

MASSEY UNIVERSITY PRESS

A netball match between Nelson and West Coast in 1947, at the 18th Dominion Tournament held in Nelson.
Netball New Zealand

Contents

The Silver Ferns celebrate winning the 2019 World Cup by beating Australia in the final by one goal.
Michael Bradley

INTRODUCTION
Rivalry, resilience and redemption

The Silver Ferns are New Zealand's national netball team. The team name originates from the silver underside of the leaves on the tree fern *Cyathea dealbata*, an iconic symbol for many New Zealand sports teams. Historically, the Silver Ferns have been one of the top two national netball teams in the world. They have qualified to compete at every World Netball Championships (initially known as the World Tournament, now World Cup) since its inauguration in 1963, and at every Commonwealth Games since the inclusion of netball in 1998. They have won the World Championships five times (1967, 1979, 1987, 2003 and 2019) and won the World Games title in 1985 and 1989. They also won gold medals at the Commonwealth Games in 2006 and 2010.

However, the 80-year history of the fierce rivalry between the Australian Diamonds and the Silver Ferns has long favoured the Australians. At the end of the 2019 season, the Australians had won 95 of the 151 international matches between the two nations, with New Zealand winning 54 and two games being drawn (see Table 1). Many of Australia's wins in title duels against New Zealand have also been heartbreakingly close. On four occasions (1963, 1991, 1999 and 2011) Australia beat New Zealand by one goal. In 1999 the Silver Ferns were the in-form team going into the World Cup, and during the final match in Christchurch they took a six-goal lead heading into the final quarter. The Diamonds fought back, and with 22 seconds left on the clock the scores were tied. Donna Wilkins (née Loffhagen) had a shot to win for the Ferns and missed. Liz Ellis regained it, the ball flew down the court in typical Australian style, and Sharelle McMahon sank the pressure shot to win the cup for the Diamonds. For the Ferns, with victory snatched away in the final seconds against their closest rivals, the one-point loss was gut-wrenching. On top of this came a double-overtime loss to the Diamonds in the 2002 Commonwealth Games final, with McMahon again shooting the winning goal.

The following year, however, the Silver Ferns won the Netball World Cup, breaking the Diamonds' 16-year winning streak and gaining redemption for the losses in 1999 and 2002. And in 2019 — by which time the Diamonds had built up another 16-year unbeaten streak — the Ferns won the World Cup again with a thrilling one-point victory in Liverpool. The Silver Ferns had been vilified in the press for their performance at the 2018 Commonwealth Games, when there were plenty of tears and questions after their 60–55 loss to Jamaica robbed them of a medal. A week earlier, they had suffered their first ever defeat to Malawi. In 2019, however, Casey Kopua (née Williams) came out of retirement, Laura Langman was finally handed an exemption from Netball New Zealand's selection policy for playing in Australia, and Katrina Rore (née Grant) returned to the team, having initially missed selection after captaining the unsuccessful 2018 Commonwealth Games campaign. Star shooter Maria Folau (née Tutaia) was also instrumental to the team's success, despite the distraction of her husband, Israel Folau's, very public sacking by the Australian Rugby Union for his comments on social media. However, it was Noeline Taurua's appointment as coach that provided the 'perfect storm', and the catalyst for what had appeared an unlikely win just months before.

Commenting on that win, netball coaching legend Dame Lois Muir opined that the 'Australians think they walk on water, but really, they were catching up all the time. New Zealand were sort of controlling that game, and that was a great feeling to have.'[1] Muir had coached the 1987 Silver Ferns to World Cup victory, redeeming the 1983 loss to Australia in Singapore. In the words of their captain, Waimarama Taumaunu, 'there was a number of us that had been to Singapore in 1983 and we'd lost and there was a strong determination that we weren't going to do that again . . . losing was not something we turned up to do'.[2] And 1987 player Leigh Gibbs (née Mills) highlighted the resilience of the team: 'The collaboration was outstanding . . . We were demanding of each other . . . it was a reflection of how hard we wanted it and how hard we worked.'[3]

Rivalry, resilience and redemption are the key themes that stand out in this book. *Will to Win* is, we hope, an insightful examination of the traditions, team culture, leadership and coaching styles that have evolved over the years through the eyes of some of the great Silver Ferns coaches and captains. Interviewees were asked to reflect upon how they heard about their selection, the team induction process, symbols, rites and rituals, values and beliefs. The emphasis on winning and the rivalry with Australia were also explored. They were also asked to highlight some of the external environmental factors — political, economic, sociocultural and technological — that have influenced the team's development.

The first section reflects on personal perspectives on netball. The second features interviews with captains and coaches over the period from 1960 to 1987. This era saw many significant changes and developments, such as the introduction of a set of international rules in 1961. In 1974 Lois Muir took over as coach, which began the most successful period in New Zealand netball's international history. The third section covers the period between 1988 and 2001, which involved rebranding and commercialisation, with a far greater involvement from sponsors. The association changed its name in 1991 and became known as Netball New Zealand, while also adopting a new logo, the silver fern, and the national team became known as the Silver Ferns. The fourth section covers the period 2002–19, which saw the transitioning of netball to athlete-centred semi-professionalism, and even full professionalism for some of the elite players. The final section covers some history of the game in New Zealand, then reflects on some of the key themes of the interviews.

TABLE 1: NEW ZEALAND VS AUSTRALIA, 1938–2019

ERA	TOTAL GAMES	NZ WINS	AUSTRALIA WINS	DRAWS	NZ WINS (%)
1938–59	4	0	4		0
1960–73	8	3	5		38
1974–87	19	9	8	2	47
1988–2001	35	10	25		29
2002–15	61	26	35		43
2016–19	24	6	18		25
1938–2019	**151**	**54**	**95**	**2**	**36**

Tech Old Girls versus St Mary's, Wellington, 1955. *Alexander Turnbull Library, EP/1955/1237-F*

PART 1

A love of netball

LANA McCARTHY

Dr Lana McCarthy has spent the past 10 years in the sport, education and coaching sector in various roles, including as a registered health and physical education teacher, a netball development officer, a regional sports advisor, and as a lecturer in physical education.

She was a netball coach for a range of high-performance New Zealand netball teams, spanning secondary school, Under 17, Under 19 and Under 23 level. She undertook research for her master's thesis with the Northern Mystics ANZ Championships netball team in 2014, on the development and importance of establishing team culture and leadership within sports teams. This led to a PhD investigating team culture, leadership and coaching styles, and the ways in which captains and coaches have constructed the culture within the Silver Ferns — the first study of its kind in New Zealand.

Players need to be able to think for themselves, make split-second decisions and act upon these decisions with confidence and self-assurance, taking responsibility for their own actions.

Like thousands of other young netball players in New Zealand, I grew up with aspirations of one day playing for the Silver Ferns. I would watch my idol Bernice Mene and hope that one day I would play goal defence for the Silver Ferns just like her. I have countless childhood memories of watching televised games of the Ferns playing against the Australian Diamonds, with victory often impossible to predict until the final seconds. I also remember being glued to the television and witnessing momentous moments in the history of the game, such as the one-goal loss to Australia in the dying seconds of the 1999 World Netball Championships in Christchurch, or the epic moment when Temepara George (now Bailey) was sent off during the final of the World Cup in 2003 — and the Silver Ferns got their revenge by reclaiming the trophy, and the title as the world's top-ranked netball team.

I began playing netball for Cornwall Street Primary School in Masterton. On cold winter Saturday mornings we played on the asphalt at the Colombo Road netball courts. The old blue pleated netball skirt came down to my knees as I ran around with my teammates, chasing and crowding the ball like bees around a honey pot. We would rotate positions every quarter and I would try my hardest to avoid the goal shoot and goal attack bib so I wouldn't have the added pressure (and embarrassment!) of trying to get the ball through what seemed then to be a ridiculously tall hoop. These early experiences would result in netball for evermore becoming my sport of choice.

When I moved to Masterton Intermediate School, I was nervous about having to trial to be placed in a netball team. The pressure of competing against others was daunting, but this was just the first of many netball trials to come. I was the only Year 7 student to make the A1 team, the rest being Year 8s. This had not happened before, and so it was a very big deal! I also have fond memories of my classroom teacher, Mr Thompson, being so proud of me. Those intermediate years also solidified my preferred playing position: a defender at heart, goal defence was where I belonged on court.

At Wairarapa College I continued to play netball. I was the first Year 11 student to make the Senior A1 team, going on to captain that team, and I was named in the Wellington Regional Talent Identification Squad. I also progressed throughout the Wairarapa representative netball age-group teams, playing for the Under 15s and Under 17s.

In my childhood and adolescent playing years, the support and encouragement of my parents was an important factor in my continued involvement in netball. They made every effort to come to nearly all my games and representative tournaments, while juggling three kids who played three different winter sports. They both also played numerous roles: supporter, manager, taxi driver, counsellor, financial backer and first-aider.

In 2005 I moved to Palmerston North to study a bachelor of sport and exercise at Massey University (and then a graduate diploma to qualify as a physical education teacher). The level of performance and competition was much higher than in small-town Masterton, and I realised very quickly that I had to work twice as hard if I wanted to play regional netball at the top level.

On the recommendation of a former Masterton teammate who was playing for the club, I trialled for Feilding Netball Club, and was selected for one of the Premier One netball teams. I felt way out of my depth and intimidated, as some of my teammates were Western Flyers netball players, who went on to get ANZ contracts and even play for the Silver Ferns. However, I also thrived on being pushed harder than I had ever been pushed before, and it was during this period that I developed the most as a player. My coach was Yvette McCausland-Durie (later the Central Pulse and Silver Ferns assistant coach), who at the time was coaching the Western Flyers team. I hung off her every word. I was in awe of her knowledge of the game and truly admired the way she formed positive relationships with her players, while also expecting a high level of work and performance.

During my first year with Feilding Netball Club, I also made the Manawatū Under 19 representative team. For the next 10 years I continued to play Premier One netball; during that time, however, I suffered a serious injury, requiring two shoulder reconstructions followed by intensive strength and rehabilitation programmes. This meant spending a few months on the bench. I never returned to full strength as a player and realised that I could no longer compete at Premier One level. It was a turning point in my career in netball and I needed to re-evaluate my involvement in the game.

A role in administration was still an option, and so I joined the club committee. I was later voted chairperson (2017–18). Although my days of competing in Premier One netball were in the past, I still wanted to play, so I joined the Feilding Reserves team, a team of former Feilding Netball Club Premier One players, playing in the grade below.

In 2018, while completing my PhD, I was a member of the Massey University Tertiary netball team that competed at the New Zealand university games in Auckland. Having always been a staunch Feilding member, it felt odd to be playing for a team that I usually played and coached against. There were many good, hard battles! I came into that team as one of the oldest players, and some of my teammates were also my students. I have such positive memories of this experience, as I was welcomed with open arms and instantly made to feel a valuable member of the team. To my surprise, this 'old girl' secured a starting position and our team went on to compete in the final against Waikato University. Ahead by one goal in the closing seconds, we showed great composure. We played the ball around, maintaining possession as the clock wound down, and went on to win the New Zealand Tertiary National Netball title.

GD

As a young netball player I was the recipient of the 'traditional' autocratic style of coaching. I was told what to do, how to perform it and when to do it in a game. My teammates and I relied heavily on the coach to provide the instructions and the game plan. When we deviated from this plan we would be thrown into a state of panic as we didn't have the skills or capability to think for ourselves, make decisions and react to challenges on court.

This was how netball was taught in those days. There was limited knowledge of coaching styles or approaches. I had never heard of concepts such as Teaching Games for Understanding or an 'empowering' approach towards coaching. It wasn't until I played under Yvette McCausland-Durie that I experienced a different style of coaching: one where players were included a lot more, were asked questions and were encouraged to think for themselves, and where the environment was competitive but you also felt at ease with your coach and your teammates.

As my playing career reached its peak, I turned my attention to coaching. I began in 2009 as coach of the Senior A1 netball team at Freyberg High School, then taking over as head coach of the Palmerston North Girls' High School Senior A1 in 2015, and working as a Manawatū representative coach from 2010 to 2019, the assistant coach of the Central Zone Under 23 netball team and other various talent identification coaching programmes run by Netball Central. In 2019 I had my first year as head coach of the Feilding A1 — the team I had played for many years prior. Still competing in the Manawatū Premier One competition, we had set the goal as a team early on in the season that we were going to win. We achieved that goal and for the first time in 10 years Feilding A1 were the Premier One netball champions. That was one of my proudest coaching moments — not because we won, but because this group of players and management was truly the most united, positive, supportive and hard-working team that I had ever had the pleasure of coaching. I was also deeply honoured to have received the Manawatū 2019 Coach of the Year award.

I'm a strong believer in the importance of using an empowering approach when coaching players and teaching students. Players should be encouraged to learn independently and to *want* to seek improvement and development in their own performances. Players need to be able to think for themselves, make split-second decisions and act upon these decisions with confidence and self-assurance, and take responsibility for their own actions.

But while I favour the empowering approach, I have also come to recognise that there's a place for both the autocratic and the empowering styles. My coaching approach has evolved over time into a more mixed coaching style, which aims to teach players to take responsibility for their performances and the decisions they make, and to learn and grow from these experiences, while also being given clear directions at times when particular technical and/or tactical aspects need to be reinforced.

My passion for netball and for coaching has been the foundation of my PhD research and now this book. I hope to have an impact on increasing the percentage of female high-performance coaches across various sporting codes in New Zealand.

I hope, too, to continue coaching for as long as possible. A coach never stops learning and must take every opportunity to grow, be open to new ideas, and be brave enough to take risks. The longer I've coached, particularly at the higher levels, the more I've come to realise how much is involved in the role. One of the key lessons I've learnt is that I don't have to pretend to know everything. It's more than okay to admit my weaknesses. It's been far more beneficial for my own growth as a coach to admit the areas I needed further development in and to be confident, not ashamed, to ask for help. When I realised this, I found myself a mentor, Nic Lush, who I continue to work with to this day. Nic has supported me, challenged me, encouraged and pushed me.

I am steadily making my way through the modules and practical observations for the Netball New Zealand Performance Coach qualification. Most recently this involved being observed by former Silver Ferns head coach Waimarama Taumaunu and, another of my childhood idols, former Silver Ferns captain and the best centre in the team's history, Sandra Edge. This was both terrifying and exhilarating!

Team culture and leadership are key themes in this book, but when I first began coaching, I had absolutely no idea what team culture was. I did not know the impact it could have on a team or how to develop it. When I completed my master's thesis I spent time with the Northern Mystics ANZ franchise team; this was my first introduction to the concept, and my growing interest in its positive or negative impact on performance motivated me to investigate the links between team culture, leadership and winning at an elite level with the Silver Ferns.

As I learnt more about team culture, I recognised its absence from my own coaching. I began to adapt what I was learning to creating a positive team culture within the Palmerston North Girls' High School Senior A1 netball team. Over the next four years the team's rituals included player/parent barbecues, presentation of team uniforms and the formal announcement of the captain. Regular team bonding sessions were part of the training calendar, and involved pizza, laser-tag and tenpin bowling — anything outside of the 'netball' environment. Team values were discussed and agreed upon as a collective, and leadership groups were established.

I found that it takes time to establish a positive team culture and I learnt not to expect a drastic change over the course of one season. I also found that one idea may work better with one group of players than with another, and that a high turnover of players from year to year has an impact. I also learnt how culture reflects the *whole* team; it takes every single member contributing and playing a role to create a positive culture.

I have been incredibly fortunate to have developed long-lasting friendships with players, other coaches and teammates. Netball has given me the opportunity to travel around the country, both as a player and as a coach, and has also allowed me to meet and interview the legends of netball and many of my childhood heroes. Most importantly, I've developed a deep respect for those who volunteer their time to coach, and not just netball. I hope that these amazing people realise the significant impact that they have, not only on the sport itself, but also on the lives of their players.

FARAH PALMER

Dr Farah Rangikoepa Palmer is Associate Dean Māori for the Massey Business School and a senior lecturer in the School of Management, Massey University. Her teaching and research focuses on sport sociology and leadership as they relate to diversity and team culture, with a particular emphasis on Māori and women. Farah played 35 tests and captained the New Zealand Black Ferns team to three consecutive Women's Rugby World Cup wins in 1998, 2002 and 2006. In 1998 she was awarded Women's Player of the Year by the NZ Rugby Football Union (NZRFU), and in 2005 she was awarded International Women's Personality of the Year by the International Rugby Board (IRB). Her work in sport and women's rugby was acknowledged in 2007 when she became an Officer of the New Zealand Order of Merit (ONZM), and she was inducted into the World Rugby Hall of Fame in 2014. Since retiring, Farah has continued in rugby in a variety of capacities, including a two-year stint coaching a women's club team. In 2016 she became the first female director on the New Zealand Rugby Board and the chair of the New Zealand Māori Rugby Board, and in 2018 she became a director of Sport NZ.[4]

High-profile female athletes and teams in New Zealand are, whether they like it or not, role models, rangatira (leaders) and kaitiaki (guardians) for future generations.

Rugby may be romantically considered New Zealand's national sport, but until recently that has only reflected the male part of our national obsession with team sports. Netball, on the other hand, has held the reputation of being New Zealand's national team sport for women, with over 300,000 participants playing some version of the game. As a Sport NZ board member, I believe any sport that encourages girls and women to be active is a good thing. With elite teams like the Silver Ferns, and the high participation rate of women and girls in the sport nationwide, netball is in a great space to continue enabling women and girls to realise their potential and enhance their well-being in and through sport and active recreation.

Netball was and always will be my first love when it comes to organised sport. As a young child, I remember three generations of women making the 40-kilometre round trip from Piopio to the Te Kuiti netball courts to watch my mum play. It was a Saturday morning ritual we all looked forward to. I'd be running along the fence line close to the courts with Nana keeping an eye on me. Meanwhile, Mum played netball enthusiastically in her pleated skirt, tie-up bib and white Bata Bullets shoes. I soon followed in her footsteps and played for our local primary school. In the 1980s my netball initiation kicked into overdrive when Silver Ferns netball stars became my idols. Lois Muir was a household name; the dynamic defensive duo of Tracey Fear and Waimarama Taumaunu inspired me (I fancied myself as a defence player back then!); the flair and spatial awareness of Rita Fatialofa, and the energy and cheekiness of Sandra Edge, the 'Margs' — Margharet Matenga and Margaret Forsyth — blew me away; and we all felt the dream of wearing the silver fern was even closer when local girl Rhonda Wilcox (née Meads) donned the black dress for Aotearoa New Zealand. The dream came even closer when fellow Piopio-ite Jenny May Clarkson (née Coffin) also became a Silver Fern from 1997 to 2002.

For me the 1990s meant a change of city and a change of sport from the round ball to the oval ball. I didn't fall out of love with netball, and always thought I'd return to the Bata Bullets someday. That day happened after retiring from rugby and having my first child. Netball seemed like the best way to get back into shape, and regain my sense of identity and feeling of camaraderie I got when playing for the Black Ferns. I also believed netball culture, with strong female engagement everywhere, would be supportive of a mum wanting to find her mojo again. Netball was a sport I could easily take my child to, where they'd be safe with many people on the sidelines volunteering to keep an eye on them. The games didn't take too long, and everyone understood what it was like to squeeze in a bit of 'me' time with a young family. I continued to play netball through both my pregnancies, and enjoy playing to this day. Some days it is a challenge to put on the netball uniform and drag the kids out the door, but the competitive spirit kicks into gear when the whistle blows and it is all on! Afterwards I feel exhilarated, exhausted and satisfied. It is important for women of all shapes, sizes, circumstances and abilities to be active, connected and energised. Perhaps that competitive spirit that comes with playing at the elite level never leaves.

Team culture and leadership

The approach to culture and leadership in the Black Ferns team was not far removed from what I had learnt through playing netball as a child and teenager. It included having clear goals, respecting the wisdom of those who have skin in the game, pushing each other to be better, encouraging a collaborative style of leadership, appreciating that a division of labour is better for the team, and celebrating that diversity brings strength. The underlying values and attributes expected in high-performance sport are often similar, yet they may be demonstrated through different rituals, artefacts, language and symbols. I'm sure the Silver Ferns over the years have adapted these 'visible' signs of team culture and leadership to reflect their core values and attitudes. It is important to note, however, that with the korowai (cloak) of mana that comes with wearing any black uniform comes great responsibility. I am a strong believer that there is often a greater expectation for female athletes and sports teams to be the moral guardians of society. It comes with gendered expectations that are still dominant in New Zealand, which are not necessarily fair or right, but are the reality in many situations.

During my first season playing rugby, I 'performed' many of the netball rituals that had become instinctive to me and which perhaps are more traditionally aligned with behaviour considered to be fair play; behaviour such as clapping when the opposition scored, going out of my way to thank the umpire and opponents, helping out players who fall or injure themselves, helping out off the field with what needed to be prepared/packed away, and generally playing fair but hard. Some of these rituals were drummed out of me, but they were always there, dormant, waiting to be reignited. There were also technical skills I gained in netball that helped me in rugby and life in general, such as effective communication (both verbal and physical), spatial awareness and vision, embracing hard work and flair, and the ability to adapt to any situation or opponent.

High-profile female athletes and teams in New Zealand are, whether they like it or not, role models, rangatira (leaders) and kaitiaki (guardians) for future generations. This leadership by example can add to an already high-pressure situation, and those who rise to that challenge, who are prepared for these expectations and are resilient can survive and increase their sphere of influence. I just hope we are wrapping enough support around our elite female athletes and teams, such as the Silver Ferns, to cope with this heightened expectation.

Times have changed a little with a move towards professionalism and greater acceptance of 'gamesmanship', but it is interesting to see how pockets of New Zealand athletes and teams are rejecting this 'win at all costs' mentality, in favour of values such as playing hard but fair, and respecting that everyone (including officials) gives 100 per cent. Yes, the game at the elite level is more physical these days (as is the case in most performance and power sports), the uniforms and rules have adapted, and competition for media attention and sponsorship is fiercer. Nonetheless, the underlying principles of teamwork, fun, the pursuit of excellence and continual improvement, resilience and determination remain relevant.

BETTY STEFFENSEN

Betty Steffensen (née Pratt) has made a significant contribution to netball. In 1979 she received the New Zealand Service Medal from the national body in recognition of 25 years of service to the game (both regionally and nationally), and she was made a life member in 1991. She also received the Queen's Service Medal (QSM) in 1990, which recognises an individual's voluntary service to the community, and the Suffrage Centennial Medal, awarded in 1993 to 500 women and men who had, by their virtues and talents, made a contribution to the rights of women in New Zealand. Betty was named vice-captain for the New Zealand team touring Australia in 1960, playing one test. She was the first Silver Fern to also become an international umpire (1973–74) and a manager of a Netball New Zealand team (1980–83).

Team culture is vital. You can have a team, a moulded team of friends, who can outplay a team of individuals, so it's the leadership that brings them all together.

I have been privileged to have had a lifetime of involvement in the most popular women's sport in New Zealand. But I found it quite daunting to be asked to write a little about my experiences, the development of the game and the changes I have seen over the past 60 years. Why? Because these alone could fill a volume!

In 1960 I was stunned to be named as one of the national netball trialists. Our team had not even been told of the forthcoming tour to Australia. The trials were to be held 10 months after the announcement, and over those 10 months, trialists received scant information as to how best prepare themselves, and had no communication with either the coach or selectors.

On Queen's Birthday Friday 1960, I travelled by train to Wellington for the trials. At their conclusion we were ushered into a little room where the announcement of the team was to take place. The Netball New Zealand president said, 'We'll announce the team now.' I had married in 1958 and I was listening intently as the names were being read out in alphabetical order. When they had gone past Pratt I assumed I had missed out (I wasn't surprised), but then they got to Steffensen — 'Oh, that's me!' It was just one of those very special moments. I could not believe my ears. Who — me? I was a country kid, only five feet and half an inch tall, playing as a goal attack/goal shooter, and one of two trialists selected from the second-grade tournament, while all of the other 19 trialists were selected from first grade! Never in my wildest dreams had I thought I'd be selected. It was only when we got home that Dad mentioned, 'They said you were vice-captain,' and I said, 'Pardon?' They did not name the captain or vice-captain when naming the team earlier. Dad had heard the radio bulletin, and he met me with a cheque for twenty pounds in his hand! (He had never given me money in his life before.)

Up until 1978 the Netball New Zealand (NNZ) executive was regionally based. This put enormous pressure on that association, which was also required to administer its own centre. Administration of sport throughout New Zealand was becoming more professional, and our Wellington-based executive took a proposal to the council for a major change to the national running of netball. The proposal suggested having an executive of seven members, spread nationwide. People had been approached to fill the appropriate positions. The proposal was accepted and took effect immediately. So began the first of my 12 years as NNZ vice-president. In 1979 the first national Under 21 team was selected to tour Australia. Dale O'Neill (now Wortman) was the sole selector coach, and I was appointed manager.

It could never have been envisaged by our early pioneers that both men and women could make a career from administration, playing, umpiring and coaching from the game of netball in today's world. I have been privileged to have had a lifetime as a volunteer in so many facets of the game at national level — namely, as Silver Fern No. 29 (1960), manager of the first Under 21 team (1979), Silver Ferns manager (1980–83), international umpire (1973–74), vice-president NNZ (1978–89), and convenor of the Life Membership Committee (1991–2012).

Team culture and leadership

Team culture is vital. You can have a team, a moulded team of friends, who can outplay a team of individuals, so it's the leadership that brings them all together. You would never consider that you were going to lose; it was 'We are here to win', and that desire was just as strong then as it is today against Australia. I have been privileged to work with a number of the Silver Fern captains and coaches who feature in this book.

LOIS MUIR

My association with our netball legend Lois Muir began when we both represented New Zealand in the 1960 team. I was later one of Lois's managers during her Silver Ferns coaching era, and we were both on the

Because of her manner, commitment, enthusiasm and dedication, Lois had total respect from her players.

NNZ executive for many years. When on tour our party consisted of 12 players, a coach, a manager and an umpire. The manager's role was to attend to all travel requirements, pair up players at accommodation, see to all personal needs of players and be the main liaison for the team. Should the players have injuries, the manager was responsible for setting up and accompanying players to appointments. I never made decisions without consultation with Lois. In my mind it was her team. She always kept buzzing, she was so enthusiastic. How she could keep that momentum going was unbelievable.

I was in awe of Lois as a coach. Because of her manner, commitment, enthusiasm and dedication, she had total respect from her players. This meant that she could demand what she wanted from them, but in such a way that the players clearly understood what was required of them — and they delivered! Her innovative ability to dream up fresh ideas that would challenge and extend her team (especially when on tour, and generally in the middle of the night with a coffee in her hand) was quite remarkable. Her desire to keep giving to the game, her enthusiasm and her drive as a coach never seemed to fade.

Lois was a hard taskmaster, but her players would do all they could for her, such was their respect. Lois would speak with the captain and the vice-captain before games — and she would speak very definitely to them if she felt there was something not right. I remember her saying to one of the defence, 'Stop getting your head down. Get your head up and watch the ball; you don't have to count the nits in your opponent's hair!'

I well remember a spectator speaking to me at the conclusion of the first indoor test match played in 1982, in Palmerston North, against Australia. She was appalled at the manner in which Lois spoke to her players during the breaks: 'Lois was extremely critical, rather than positive,' she said, 'it's not the way to coach at all!' I assured her that the players would die for Lois and fully understood what was required of them. I may add that we won that match in 1982, as well as many others in that era. It was not uncommon at an after-match discussion for players to ask Lois what she had meant about a 'comment' during a break, and for her to answer, 'Did I really say that?' amid much laughter.

LYN GUNSON

We had outstanding leadership models, and one of them was Lyn Gunson. She was an excellent captain of the Silver Ferns, and soon after my appointment as manager I was delighted to receive a letter from her saying, 'Welcome to our team, but if you can't laugh don't come'! Lyn was a staunch and dynamic leader — very technical, and analytical in everything that she thought about the game, how she played the game and how she saw players as role models. She was serious but caring, and a great example, especially for the younger members of the team.

LEIGH GIBBS

Leigh was a great team player in that 1981–83 team. Her effort, attitude, determination and dedication were so evident in whatever she did. Her disappointment in losing the World Tournament in Singapore in 1983 has stayed with me to this day. Later in the day, after we lost the final, I caught up with her lying on her bed. Though she was devastated, she said to me, 'I'm going to come back in four years' time and we will win the Worlds.' True to her word, she was back, but as captain — and yes, they did win! But hers was not just a natural skill: it was absolute hard work, effort and desire; she was another amazing role model.

The people who brought netball to New Zealand and spread it through the country were truly committed enthusiasts. Ever since then, we have been extremely blessed to have incredibly capable role models in all facets of the game. It is hard to imagine that the game of netball as we know it today has developed from such small beginnings. This book is important as it provides a record of some of the legends of the game over the past 60 years, and their insights into the team culture and leadership of the team will be particularly valuable for future players and coaches to enhance the possibility of winning.

In 1967 the New Zealand netball team, coached by Taini Jamison and captained by Judy Blair, won the second World Netball Tournament, beating Australia 40–34.
National Archives of Australia

PART 2

Nurturing and creating a team culture 1960–1987

Between 1960, when New Zealand re-entered international competition for the first time in 12 years, and 1987, when they won the World Championships for the third time, the Silver Ferns established a strong team culture. The core features of this culture — pride in being selected for the national team; accepting players for who they were as people, regardless of ethnicity and personality quirks; a strong work ethic at training; and a 'get on with it' philosophy to dealing with problems — endure to this day.

The team culture in this era was strongly influenced by the amateur status of the sport. For much of the period, financial constraints made it hard for the national team to get together prior to playing test matches, so there was little time for new players to be inducted or for lengthy discussion of team values. Nevertheless, coaches, managers, captains and senior players were clear in their expectations, and team culture was largely communicated through leading by example. With little media coverage of netball until the 1980s, players tended to meet each other through playing at national tournaments. Selection for the national team was a prized honour because, outside of World Championships, test matches were infrequent. In these circumstances, the black dress with the silver fern held a particular significance, because there were no replica uniforms made: those who wore it had earned it.

Teams had to be self-reliant. Whereas present-day international teams have a small army of support staff, including specialist coaches, medical staff and a management team, New Zealand netball teams of this era comprised a manager, the coach and the players, so keeping fit called for self-discipline. Moreover, those players, coaches and managers were unpaid; indeed, on some occasions they needed to contribute personally towards their travelling expenses. Despite these challenges, the Silver Ferns always had high expectations regarding their performance. While they were amateur in the sense that they were unpaid athletes, they were highly professional in their approach to the game.

TABLE 2: NEW ZEALAND VS AUSTRALIA, PRE-1960

YEAR	EVENT	NZ SCORE	AUS SCORE	WINNER
1938	First international in Australia	11	40	AUS
1948	Aus tour to New Zealand	16	27	AUS
1948	Aus tour to New Zealand	13	44	AUS
1948	Aus tour to New Zealand	22	44	AUS

TABLE 3: NEW ZEALAND VS AUSTRALIA, 1960–87

YEAR	EVENT	NZ SCORE	AUS SCORE	WINNER
1960	New Zealand tour to Aus	49	40	NZL
1960	New Zealand tour to Aus	39	44	AUS
1960	New Zealand tour to Aus	45	46	AUS
1963	1st World Tournament	36	37	AUS
1967	2nd World Tournament	40	34	NZL
1969	Tour to New Zealand	39	49	AUS
1969	Tour to New Zealand	43	39	NZL
1971	3rd World Tournament	42	48	AUS
1975	4th World Tournament	34	34	DRAW
1979	5th World Tournament	36	38	AUS
1981	Tri-Test Series	37	32	NZL
1981	Tri-Test Series	48	29	NZL
1981	Tri-Test Series	37	34	NZL
1982	Tour to New Zealand	54	41	NZL
1982	Tour to New Zealand	53	52	NZL
1982	Tour to New Zealand	28	33	AUS
1983	6th World Tournament	42	47	AUS
1985	Australia Games	27	27	DRAW
1985	Australia Games	31	27	NZL
1985	World Games	39	37	NZL
1986	Tri-Test Milo Series	27	37	AUS
1986	Tri-Test Milo Series	27	33	AUS
1986	Tri-Test Milo Series	27	30	AUS
1986	Prudential Cup	19	35	AUS
1986	Prudential Cup	19	31	AUS
1986	Prudential Cup	31	28	NZL
1987	7th World Championships	39	28	NZL

N.
Z.
BASKETBALL
COACH
1967

TAINI JAMISON

Taini Jamison ranks among the most successful Silver Ferns coaches, winning 90 per cent (18 wins out of 20 matches) of the games in which she coached the team. She became the team's third coach, from 1967 to 1971, and in 1967 was the first to coach a New Zealand team to victory in a Netball World Cup. In 1996 this World Cup-winning team were inducted into the New Zealand Sports Hall of Fame.

In the build-up tour ahead of the 1971 World Tournament in Jamaica, the team was away for nearly four months. The Silver Ferns were runners-up, losing to Australia 42–48 in the decisive round-robin match.

After finishing with the Silver Ferns, Taini returned to Rotorua to coach and was president of Rotorua Netball from 1981 to 2001. Her contribution to netball was recognised with an OBE in 1994 and induction into the Aotearoa Sports Hall of Fame, which celebrates outstanding Māori achievement in sport, in 2006. Further accolades came from New Zealand Netball with the inauguration of the Taini Jamison Trophy in 2008. This trophy is contested between the Silver Ferns and touring international teams other than Australia. She is also a Netball New Zealand life member.[5]

A key theme that Taini demonstrated in her coaching was a shared-leadership approach in which she encouraged all her players to have their say in what occurred in the team. She valued the contribution of her players and involved them regularly in the decision-making process. She was a clear fan of using an empowerment approach, to which her players seem to have responded well.

The Silver Ferns today need a bit more mongrel. They're too nice, some of them.

In the 1960s things were so different. There were no coaching awards at that time, so when they were scouting for the New Zealand team, all they had to go on was how a coach had performed in her own area. National coaches were elected at the annual netball meeting, and voted in by all the representatives from the different counties. The team was picked by three selectors — one had to be the coach. They held trials over a weekend. That was it; the team was chosen at those trials. There was no induction, and the team didn't meet again until they were about to leave New Zealand.

We didn't have any practices; and it was all done by letter! Everything had to be done in that week or so before we left. We needed uniforms; everything had to be set in place, and it was a traumatic time. I knew a lot of those players because we played against them for years at New Zealand tournaments, but to get together as a group was quite different. We had to bond in those few days before we left the country for Australia.

We didn't have all that much money, so everything was done on a shoestring. When we went to Perth we all had to pay $200 each. We were given a uniform and a jersey and a blazer. We were able to keep the blazer, but we had to give the jersey back. And you had to wear whatever uniform the manager told you to wear. When we went from our hotel out to the courts, we took a taxi and the manager had to keep tabs on how much she paid for it. Everything had to be accounted for. The coach was also the trainer; we didn't have a separate trainer, we didn't have a nutritionist, we didn't have anyone to look after injuries — no physio. The manager had to take the injured away to the doctor or to the hospital; we had nobody else to do that.

The manager also had most of the say about who played. She had the right to say no, you can't play that player, she's not ill or she is ill, and she's hurt. As coach, I had no say as to the final team. The only person who was allowed to speak to the press was the manager. The players and I were not allowed to talk to any press at all.

There were only 10 players, a manager and a coach; that was it. Quite often we'd go and practise, and meanwhile the manager would go off to buy our lunch and bring it back to the court. Each person had a small amount of money given to them daily, which was next to nothing, really. The girls couldn't go off and buy themselves things to eat. We were lucky we survived. These days, they're in hotels, they're looked after. If they get hurt, they come straight off and they have physios fixing them up. A nutritionist will make sure they have all the right foods to eat. It's completely different.

Another difference between now and then is that we had to play outdoors in all weathers, and nowadays, of course, they can change players whenever they like. We couldn't do that; we couldn't say, 'Oh my gosh, she's not doing what I want her to do,' and take her off, put in somebody else. You could only swap players if somebody got hurt.

One thing that I made sure they did was go in pairs and watch the other games. A lot of the girls wanted to come straight back to the hotel, but they would go and sit and watch other games to make sure that they knew what to do when they played them. I don't know whether they do that now: they just seem to play a game, get dressed and go off.

I was voted in and selected as coach in 1967 because I had had such success with the Rotorua team at the New Zealand National Tournament. A lot of people didn't agree with what I did with my team, but it seemed to work. My team were used to playing a zoning game, marking the space on court instead of the person. It was a game most other teams didn't know. That's why we were so successful. I introduced it into the New Zealand team through my two defenders, who were from Rotorua. They helped coach the other players in playing that zoning style. They're still playing a type of zoning game today, but it's different; and, of course, the woman-to-woman game that Australia plays is really top-notch. We really need to teach both; our players need to learn the ins and outs of one-on-one defence. It's a good thing that some of our people are going over to Australia and learning that style.

Team culture

The New Zealand team in 1967 had known each other for years, but not intimately. They knew each other's strengths and weaknesses. The captain at the time, Judy Blair, had competed at a New Zealand tournament around aged 15. I'd known her for quite a while, but not as a team member or someone that I had previously coached. She was a good leader, and she had good back-up from her other Canterbury and South Island players.

The team we picked that year was a real New Zealand team because there were five North Island players (one from the Far North, one from Auckland, three from Rotorua) and five South Island players. The three from Rotorua were two defence players and a shooter. That helped with binding the team and the girls getting to know each other really well. Joan Harnett and Mirth Solomon (née Te Moananui) had been in the first New Zealand team to go to England in 1963, so they'd known each other for a while.

Most of the players were New Zealand European. The only Māori girls were Tilly Vercoe and Mirth Solomon. Tilly, Mirth and Billie Irwin had played together for years, those three, against and with each other, so they were very close. They trained together every morning before school. The bond was there for them, and also for the two or three from Christchurch, who would also train together. They used to train with Sam Lewis [lecturer in physical education] at Canterbury University. He was very good; he made sure they were doing what they were supposed to be doing.[6]

We did a lot of talking and the whole team contributed. They all had their say as to what they thought should happen, and they all had input into what we were doing. I just had to set down the rules of what to do, but they were players that had been playing at top levels for many years, so they really didn't need much grooming to get them in the right area. They all trained very well together; they helped each other and there was no friction at all. They gelled as a team because they were seasoned players. Some had played at five, six or seven New Zealand tournaments. They enjoyed each other's company off the court, too. They were supportive of each other all the time and whatever they did they tried to do together; nobody went off and did their own thing.

Therefore, it was just a matter of lifting them to the next level when they went to the World Tournaments. The majority of them didn't really know what it was all about. The only ones with world team experience were Joan and Mirth. Judy Blair was not in that first New Zealand team that went to the first World Tournament. They made the transition pretty easily. As a team we went away calling ourselves 'net basketballers'. It wasn't until the tournament in 1971 that they changed it to 'netball'.

Leadership

Leadership was very important. I'm a fan of making the leader in the centre court so that she can control both ends of the court as well as the middle. She's the one who does the leading, because she can talk to both ends. But there were actually several leaders on the court: there was somebody in the defence area who was doing a lot of the leading and somebody in the shooting end who was a leader, too. They're the ones that really held that team together. They made suggestions, and they all had their input after the game as to what they felt should have happened or didn't happen.

As management, we were open to anything that was suggested by the players. The main thing was, we set our goals: everybody had to know who would get what pass and that they were either on attack or on defence. If you were on attack you knew where the ball was going, then you had to defend your partner, so that the gap was there for the players to receive the ball where we wanted them to receive it. It was quite a complicated thing, but after doing it several times and practising day after day it became second nature. Everybody knew, for example, who was going to get the pass: I've got to stand this side of my partner to defend her, so my partner can't go out and then set the pass; it's going to go there. You became defenders as well as attackers, which is something that we've lost. They're not doing the defending; they're defending when they're receiving the ball. I can see them doing that now: they're doing a lot of defending when they are about to receive the ball, but they're not doing it when the ball is in play around the circle; they're not doing their job as a defender as well. So you're not just on attack. Some of them think they are just attacking and they need to get the ball to you-know-who, get their space to get the ball, but they're not thinking about their defending skills.

In terms of my coaching style, I would tell them what I wanted. One night, when we played Trinidad and had to stop them getting the ball

From left: Casey Kopua, Taini Jamison and Laura Langman, with the Taini Jamison Trophy, contested between the Silver Ferns and touring international teams other than Australia. *Michael Bradley*

into the shooting area, I said to my defence, go and practise and make sure that you know what you're doing in that defence area. Then I went back and watched, and I can remember Mirth saying, 'We were there until nine o'clock one night; there was Taini up there doing nothing, and we were down here working out what to do the next day!' But it worked, because the next day they came out firing and did whatever they had been practising the night before. I didn't like to force anybody to do anything. It's just a matter of working it out and saying, if this happens, what will happen next? Where are you going? If you get the ball here, where are you going next? They had to find the gaps for themselves. I never told them; and they never, ever got told off. Most of them were seasoned players and they knew what was wrong, and they had to fix it up themselves.

I involved the players. Quite often I would say, you defence go over there and work out something, and you shooters work out what you want to do. The defence would then try to break up what the shooters had worked out and the shooters had to play against what the defence had worked out. So that's what I did with both ends of the court. With the centre court, you've got to be able to drive the ball down and get it to your shooters, so those players had to get it cleanly through the centre. Then they had to make sure that they were backing up the ball carrier. These were just simple things, and they did a lot of it on their own.

My job was to make sure I had the players on paper. Our sessions were around where to stand, where to go, how to defend the pass. If they wanted the ball, if it was their time to receive the pass, they had to stand in a position where it was easier for them to get the pass, either in the centre or on the side. I worked things out on paper first and then we tried them out on court. That's what we practised. It was more or less what we were used to doing at home, I suppose, and it worked, because we had very few injuries.

One of our things was that you passed the ball and then you ran, but you had to make sure you knew where the ball was. If you look at some of the players these days they pass the ball, they throw it backwards and then run back to their position with their back to the ball! If somebody wanted to pass to them they would be passing to their backs. It was just basic training that you made sure you kept your eye, your peripheral vision, where you could sight the ball, so you knew where you had to go to get it or to defend it; but these days . . .?

Emphasis on winning

In the 1967 final round-robin match, we played Australia and beat them by six or so. For me, that was the game that counted and the one I got most enjoyment out of. In the loss to Australia in 1971, the team I would have liked to put on didn't get put on. So it was a disappointment to lose that game. We could have won it, should have won it — but that's how it goes. One particular person who didn't get on the court would have gone out there and died for us. Never mind; that's all history now. They were typical Australians: they like to win, and they hate to lose. Well, so do we: we hate to lose, too. The Australians have harder training. Our training was done at home that first time when we won over in Perth. The Christchurch girls and the Southland girls, they all had to train in their own areas, and it wasn't until we got together that they trained as a team.

The Silver Ferns today need a bit more mongrel. They're too nice, some of them. Australians, when they're losing, that's when they're most dangerous. They dig their heels in and they get after that ball. They go get that ball, come hell or high water — and that's the difference. Whereas our girls think, can they get that ball; shall I go, shall I not? By that time, it's too late.

The 1971 team en route to Jamaica for the third World Cup, held in Kingston. Taini Jamison (coach) is far left and Betty Steffensen (manager) is fifth from left. *Netball New Zealand*

JOAN HARNETT

As a Canterbury player, Joan Harnett was selected for the New Zealand teams that contested World Tournaments in 1963, 1967 and 1971. She won 26 caps and was named by the Australian media as player of the tournament at the 1967 Netball World Cup in Perth, which New Zealand won. She was captain of the 1971 team, but retired in 1974 and went on to coach the Canterbury team. One of New Zealand's finest players, she also received extensive publicity because of her glamorous appearance.

In 1999 she was selected in the 'dream team' of the previous 75 years and was named player of the century. Joan has consistently been an advocate for netball. She has been openly critical of the lack of media coverage of netball and advocated greater coverage in television and print media. She was one of the first players to write a column on netball, which appeared in the national newspaper *Truth*. Outside of netball, she has had a successful career in business, being one of the first women to qualify as a real estate agent.

In her interview, Joan spoke of her competitive nature. In her words, 'You don't go out there just to play nice netball; you go out there to win.' She also talked about the rivalry with Australia and how they had more of a 'killer instinct' compared to the New Zealanders — and how she had 'the same tenacious and positive attitude as they had'. The Diamonds, she says, 'are so determined, and it's bred in them'.

Even though it had been many years since Joan had played for and captained the New Zealand netball team, her passion for the game shone as strongly as ever as she recalled her time representing New Zealand in the Silver Ferns. The key themes that stood out were the immense sense of pride in being selected for the team, and the sense of legacy she felt at representing those who had played before her. It was clearly very important to her that she was always well presented when wearing the New Zealand uniform and silver fern symbol.

You always had to take pride in the way you looked, pride in the way you played.

I began my playing years when the game was called basketball. I played right through from about the age of 12. It was always my big love. When I finished school, I played for the Sacred Heart team, now called Hearts. From there I was chosen for the New Zealand trials in 1963. It was always netball for me. I would watch the senior girls and see them all playing so well and I used to aspire to be like them. It's always been my love to get to the top. I am very competitive — I like to win, and hate to lose.

My mother played hockey for Southland. She did play basketball [netball] but preferred hockey. We were the start of netball becoming well known in my era. We never managed to attract TV exposure in the beginning, and when we did it was 10 minutes' coverage at half-time of a local rugby match.

To get selected was amazing because I had just started playing representative netball and was selected for the Canterbury team. I then trialled for the New Zealand team. I aspired to be there, and I was absolutely thrilled to have made it because there had been many other great players that had been there before me and played in my position. There was no induction: it was really straight into the thick of it.

Team culture

If you haven't got a team that has a good culture and a good team spirit, knowing or thinking the same way, then you haven't got a winning team. That's always been the hardest part in selecting seven players with the same values, because everybody is different. Some people don't put as much pressure or emphasis on making a mistake. I would always say if you make a mistake (and everyone makes a mistake at some stage) then you do your best to make up for it — you either got an intercept, or a tip which absolved your mistake — that's the way it always was in my day.

The team culture and spirit were good all the way through; probably the best was when we won in 1967. That was the first time New Zealand had won and we were all of the same frame of mind. Good, competitive team players all presenting well and extremely proud of playing for New Zealand. Playing in my first New Zealand team in 1963, we were beaten 37–36 by Australia. I've never forgotten that. My team determined we would reverse the outcome next time we played Australia!

GA

We weren't called the Silver Ferns then; things were a little different. That's why I wanted the [national] flag changed. I thought it was a wonderful opportunity to get New Zealand on board, because people recognise the fern as being the symbol of New Zealand. I thought that would have been absolutely so appropriate: it didn't matter which one as long as the fern was on it. I remember carrying the flag when we were in Jamaica in 1971 and we had just lost the final by six. I remember thinking ours looked exactly the same as everyone else's and why couldn't we have something of our own? I've always admired the Canadian flag with the maple leaf on it; it is so distinctive. It belongs to them, and we should have something that belongs to us and tells everybody that we are from New Zealand. We were only named the Silver Ferns in later days — after I had finished. I much prefer the Silver Ferns name.

We were always proud. You always had to take pride in the way you looked, pride in the way you played and pride in knowing you went out to play with a positive attitude. So to me, pride was probably the biggest thing because that covered such a lot. If you don't have pride, you don't have that killer instinct. I should have been an Australian because I had the same tenacious and positive attitude that they had, an approach which New Zealand players generally did not possess. You don't go out there just to play nice netball, you go out there to win. If anyone says otherwise they are wrong!

There was a time in later years when New Zealand wasn't doing very well. The girls were being told (and I couldn't believe it) to go out there and just enjoy it — that it doesn't matter about the winning. You don't do that at top-level netball; you might do that with 10- and 11-year-olds just to get them into the way of the game, but you certainly don't do that at top level. That's why we lost our way for a few years. We needed to get that killer instinct, just like the Aussies. If you're getting away with something on the court, you keep doing it, and if the others are getting away with it then you do it as well. It's tit for tat, and all's fair in love and war!

Leadership

Without leadership, everyone would be doing their own thing. You must have someone who takes control and commands (in a nice way, though, so as not to offend). That leader must earn the trust and respect of the team players — a must if you want to succeed. I had the respect of people in Canterbury due to my netball background and I became only the third woman in Christchurch to go into real estate, believe it or not! Having been a leader in netball allowed me to forge a new career.

There were a number of us that went through with the Ferns who aspired to become the New Zealand coach at some time or other. But the head coaching role was held by Lois Muir, who was fully ensconced in the position and she wasn't budging. None of us really got the opportunity to take on the Silver Ferns, which is what I would have liked to have done. There was no room at the top, whereas today coaches turn over every three years or so. They might get another year or two, like other sports, but they turn over much more quickly. Depending on the successes the team has had, if you're not performing, you're not doing your job. The thinking of the netball hierarchy in those days was not what it is today. Everything is run a lot better now; like the netball board. We were the pioneers, really, when we started our netball lives.

When I went to Dunedin from Christchurch in 1996, I was asked if I would coach the university B side, who had lost their position in the A grade and gone down to the B grade. I had decided that I wouldn't coach anymore. I had coached Canterbury for two years and had opened my own real estate business, which was a full-time occupation. However, I said I would come down and give them a few tips — well, of course, they were great girls, so I ended up taking them. I had no stars in that team, not one person who was known to anybody. I had to get them into a good team structure as quickly as possible because our first game up in grading was to play the team that had won the championship the year before, the top team. My team was very nervous and intimidated taking on the top team, so I had to reassure them. I said I wouldn't be standing here coaching if I did not think they had it in them to beat this team. I believed that they could, as I'd been coaching them the way the game should be played, making the ball work for them, and they were all doing it well. I had every confidence in them and they won! They did what I told them to do and they could see why. They understood the drills I had introduced to make the ball work for them through the court. The drills might be seen as boring, but often you must repeatedly do the same thing over and over again to establish a pattern.

The coaching wasn't as strict in past days. We had Taini [Jamison] twice; she's a great lady and she does know her netball, but she probably could have been a bit stricter. If you wanted to change somebody on the court because it wasn't working, a player should be told 'You will go there', not asked 'Will you go there?' The coach does have the final say because she's the person who's really in charge of the team. Taini was excellent in that she always spoke with me and we discussed who we both thought would go on the court against a certain team. We got along really well, but she needed to be a wee bit tougher. Then I'm probably a bit tougher than she is; that's the way it is.

Her coaching style let you do your own thing. She let natural talent flow, and you've got to do that. You can't just stop people's abilities when that's what they've been chosen to do. For example, Sandra Edge played that lovely flowing, straight-through game and everyone loved her because she was allowed to do it. The only thing you can do with those sorts of people is perhaps point out you can't do it all the time, because there are times where you've got to pull your horns in. There are times when you've got to play slowly because it suits another team to play fast. The coaching today is much more in-depth.

As captain of Canterbury for 10 years and then captain of the Silver Ferns, I usually deliberated with the coach over which players should be on the court against a particular team. When that was decided, the team was informed who was going to play, which strategies would be used and the reasons why particular players had been chosen. In the first two World Games there were no substitutions other than for injury. So it was only in [my] last World Tournament [as captain] where we were allowed to substitute, but only at half-time and with permission from the other team coach. These days, substitutions are the norm, so it makes for better play and teamwork. Subbing gives the coach and the team the opportunity to experiment with different players in different positions and to replace a player who isn't performing or gelling with other players — it makes a coach's job easier.

As a captain it's your leadership ability to get people onside with you and get the best from them, that is the chief part of the captaincy role. Each player reacts differently to different ways and different styles, so it is most important to get everybody onside and mould them into a team with a strong structure. I believe that this was one of my strengths as captain. I was able (with my court vision) to help players maintain the team structure, which eliminated most errors. New team members had strong inductions into team play and weren't just thrown into the game without training. We would often use a half-court drill to work new players into the pattern of play. Sometimes I would take my goal shooter through different techniques with just the two of us using the circle. It is also important that a captain maintains respect from the players off the court, so you must be a good role model.

Emphasis on winning

Every team player must take the court with the will to win and be determined for the full game time, even if the team is leading strongly. When the team experiences a loss you keep thinking about what you could have done to turn the tide of play. The reason for the loss might only have been one unfortunate incident — a contentious umpiring decision, a bad pass, a step or a missed goal that turns the tide just at the wrong time. One bad decision or error can change the outcome of the game. Players must accept the incident, move on with play, and resolve to keep on in a winning attitude.

When we beat Australia in 1967, this was the most momentous win for me, as we had been beaten once before by Australia by one goal. It was always the same when we played for Canterbury and the Australia team visited and played the different provinces. Canterbury beat Australia several times over these visits. I hated losing, because I had aspirations to captain a world-winning team. I never did achieve my ambition because

It's always been my love to get to the top. I am very competitive — I like to win, and hate to lose.

in 1971 in Jamaica we lost the final game to Australia. Our midcourt play had broken down, and of course substitutions were not allowed during the quarters so we were unable to introduce another player. We didn't lose by much, but that was my most disappointing loss.

The Australian players are so determined and it's bred in them. Sport was instituted way back, and players were trained how to think and play. That was the culture there: they went out to win! Whereas the New Zealand culture was not nearly as strong. Australia also had a greater number of players from which to choose their national team. Even so, we held our own pretty well, considering we have only a quarter of the number of players that they have. New Zealand can be proud of their achievements over the years.

Environmental factors

There have been changes to the game over the years. I never played the nine-a-side, which finished just before me — three people in each area. In 1963 there were no interceptions and players weren't allowed to retrieve the ball if it went out of court. If a shot was missed at goal and it went out of court, you just had to let it go. You couldn't jump up in the air and deflect the ball back. If the goal was missed the defender just stood outside and threw the ball in.

Our games in the three World Tournaments that I played in were all held outside in the open air. Towards the end of my career we used to play in the army barracks in Christchurch when Australia came to play Canterbury or New Zealand. We would play on a hard concrete floor. You didn't have the comfort, but you didn't have the wind. You certainly didn't have the pleasure of playing on the lovely sprung floors like they do today. That's why the games have become much more vigorous and competitive, because you couldn't play that way in our day as there would have been too many injuries.

When we played against the West Indian countries, they were very, very physical. They would stand on your foot so you couldn't jump, or they'd shove you so that you would go over the line when you shot a goal, or if you went to catch the ball you'd be bumped out of the way. That sort of thing now is not nearly as noticeable. Even though they are very energetic and vigorous, you just don't get away with things like that now, and of course the umpires weren't as astute in those days either. Now we've got very qualified umpires, so the games are more closely contested and monitored.

We had to contend with a lot more than what they do these days because we didn't get treated properly for injuries, we didn't have the right shoes, and we were playing on those hard surfaces. A lot of the girls have latterly had back disc and knee and hip replacements, caused by playing on unsatisfactory surfaces and pounding their bodies. I've been a bit lucky: I have a suspect knee but I'm managing on it and I play a lot of tennis now. So I'm still playing, which is really good, because it keeps me fit and my body in shape. Today the girls have physios, hot baths, cold baths, massages; they have great shoes and clothes, and they look tremendous. You can be really proud of them; they look so good. They are beautiful girls.

GA

Politics was an issue. In the early 1970s South Africa had been embargoed as they didn't have any indigenous South Africans in their teams. This affected world netball as well, because all of the other nations, like the West Indies and Singapore — or it might have been Japan — said that if South Africa were allowed to come to the 1971 World Tournament then they would not play. It was a political situation.

GA

In terms of media, we were very fortunate in Christchurch. We had the *Press*, which was right behind Canterbury, and we got the best newspaper coverage of any city in New Zealand when we had our Saturday tournament games. They really looked after us, so I always acknowledged the *Press* because without them we wouldn't have achieved as much as quickly. Without them the public would never have had the opportunity to see what a great game netball was and what a great spectacle it was to watch. Without them we probably wouldn't have done as well. They did us proud.

I used to write for *Truth* when I was coaching. It was after I finished playing and I used to really enjoy that because I was able to voice my opinion on matters important to me. With a lack of coverage on television, though, people didn't get to see our games live. If it had been featured on TV, people would have thought, oh what a great game! We missed out on the spectacle of the crowd coming to watch a game. I used to say to the media, why aren't you giving us TV coverage? I said the public don't even know what it's like because you won't even give them a look-in. It was exactly like that, and now look what we've got! Fantastic. We really fought for that media coverage in those years, particularly for television. Look what we've got with the tennis at the moment; imagine if you didn't have tennis! Rugby was the game then, and we were second-rate citizens when it came to the media covering women's sport. You were lucky if God gave you better looks than a few others as it helped get a little more TV and media coverage.

Skellerup, who made our shoes for us, were really good sponsors. They wanted to use me to promote their Netqueen shoes. When we finally got a bit of TV coverage they wanted to do an ad with me playing in their shoes. But the netball association said no, it's a team game and you can't just pick out one person. So all I had was my foot on TV! The netball hierarchy didn't think that netball was ever going to need sponsorship, which was a ridiculous statement.

GA

Ethnicity? We had different ethnicities in all the teams I played in. There was Mirth Solomon, Frances Wiringi [now Webster], Tilly Vercoe and Rebecca Faulkner [née Chaplow]. They were great girls and we all got on like a house on fire. There was no thought of any differences as we all played the same sort of game — and if we didn't, we made sure that we did. We looked after each other.

LOIS MUIR

Dame Lois Muir was born in 1935. She represented New Zealand in two sports: the New Zealand women's basketball team from 1952 to 1962 and the New Zealand women's netball team between 1960 and 1963. She was also head coach of the Silver Ferns for 15 years from 1974 to 1988, finishing with a record of 91 wins, 10 losses and six draws.[7] During this period, the Silver Ferns won the World Championships gold in 1979 (jointly with Australia and Trinidad and Tobago), lost to Australia in 1983, but were successful in winning in 1987: 'This team knew where it wanted to be . . . They didn't want to be second to Australia again.'

Her achievements in netball were recognised with the award of an OBE in 1984 and induction into the New Zealand Sports Hall of Fame in 1993. In 2004 she was appointed a Distinguished Companion of the New Zealand Order of Merit, and granted the title of Dame in 2009.[8]

For many of us when we think of Lois Muir, we think of her long-standing involvement and her outstanding contribution to netball, helping to pave the way for future players and coaches, and playing a significant role in establishing netball as New Zealand's number-one female sport.

For her part, Lois recalls the immense pride that she felt in being selected for the first national team to play seven-a-side, the same rules as the rest of the world. She speaks, too, of the importance of team culture and leadership ('they're all leaders in different ways on the field'), but equally important was her coaching style. She admits she was mean to her players at times, but she still loved and had great belief in them. She was both authoritative and empowering in her approach. Her philosophy was that her players had to own what they wanted to achieve. 'The coach never discovers the player; they only help them discover themselves.'

I'm passionate about the game — I always have been.

The selection of a national team in 1960 was an enormous step forward for netball in New Zealand, and only came about because of a fundamental change in how the game was played here. We didn't play the same game as everyone else. Netball in New Zealand was nine-a-side and we were the only country that played that way. Everyone else played seven-a-side. The courts were three metres wider than they are now, and three players were locked in every third. The New Zealand team picked in 1938 had gone to Australia and played some games using their rules, and an Australian team came to New Zealand in 1948 and three tests were held on grass. The test in Dunedin was played in the middle of Forbury Park racetrack and they tried to mix the rules from both countries.

During most of my playing career the best I could do was represent the South Island playing the North Island because there were no New Zealand teams. In 1959 a group of very clever and forward-thinking administrators persuaded the New Zealand netball community (or, rather, took them kicking and screaming) to play seven-a-side. If they hadn't made the change to the seven-a-side game, we would never have played at the World Tournament in 1963, so these players were really ahead of their time. It was very exciting to be in that first New Zealand team touring another country playing seven-a-side. Every court had to be made narrower, however with fewer players on court there was more room to move. Those of us that had played basketball — Pam Barham, June Waititi [now Dame June Mariu] and I — were more accepting of the new rules and saw the opportunity of the increased space more quickly than some of the others, who were used to that stilted sort of a game where you were locked in the thirds. That 1960 team that toured Australia had a lot of people in there that had both played netball for a long time and accepted the seven-a-side parameters a lot better. It was amazing, and we felt we were making history: it was more than just playing for our country; it was being able to play the rest of the world for the first time.

Team culture

I felt there was more of a team culture when Joyce McCann was the manager of the 1963 trip to the World Tournament in England. We had a couple of board members who travelled on the ship with us. We stayed in a university hostel and it was an amazing experience to have the other teams in our dormitory. We had guitars and always had things going on. We entertained ourselves and seemed self-contained, whereas a lot of other countries were looking for someone to entertain them. It felt like we had everybody migrating to us; they thought we were great. We would have teams supporting us even though they had been knocked out; they felt they had been our friends. It was the New Zealand way that we accepted anyone for who they were. It was a new experience, and was very important for the team culture.

There was no induction into the team. You went to trials, and then they named a team and you were told you were coming back to do a few days' training before you toured. It was an interesting exercise in 1960 because it was the first time a New Zealand netball team had travelled overnight — we took a sleeper train from Melbourne to Adelaide. When you're away on tour you get to know people in the team, understand differences and work together. That's most important. It's when you care for each other that you really are successful on the court. You don't have to live in everyone's pocket when you're off the court, but you do have to accept that we are all different. It was good for me to learn those things as a player.

Later, when I was coaching, the philosophy of the Netball New Zealand executive, who held the power and the money (there wasn't a lot of it), was to allow about nine days of training before a test match. So you really had to start from scratch. Up until 1983 I was allowed only 10 players, with no subs (you could replace somebody if there was a really bad injury, but they could not come back on again).

In 1963 the members in the team didn't really know each other until we

The 1963 New Zealand netball team (Lois Muir is second from right) hold their kiwi and doll mascots as they board the ship bound for the inaugural World Tournament in Eastbourne, England. New Zealand were runners-up at the event. *Netball New Zealand*

got on the ship. We got to Auckland for training but I really only knew the other team members from playing against them in Canterbury or in the North vs South matches. It was like that in the early New Zealand teams that I coached. I would get a group together that I'd never had much to do with. I became the sole selector and coach, and I quite liked that because I was in control of selection and the chop marks were on my neck if I didn't succeed. Otherwise, you had people lobbying for players, so you just picked the team, gave the list to somebody, and they read it out in the room. The ones who weren't in went out, and the ones that were in stayed and I said hello to them, and that was it.

We had a team symbol, a little Māori doll in traditional costume, which came with us most of the time. She went with us to the first World Tournament in England in 1963. I missed the next two World Tournaments, so I'm not sure what happened to that doll.

At the 1963 World Tournament, we had to put items on at the concert for all teams, so we were doing poi while some were canoe rowing in the background, although a few of us were not very good with our timing. We were also doing the haka in those days. June Waititi's brother had taken us for some training that was acceptable for females, as the haka was typically only performed by males. We did a lot of Māori songs and action songs for concert performances. Mind you, we had six weeks on the ship getting there so we had a lot of time to practise, and do some netball training of course. When I was coaching, we always had a strong element of Māori culture in our team when we went away, which was extremely important to us, and we always carried a fluffy kiwi with us.

Leadership

Leadership is very important. In 1975 I stood the captain off in a game because she wasn't playing well. She had an injury, but she wouldn't tell me about it because it was her final series. I was new to coaching and I wanted the respect from my players, so I had to put the best team on. I carried that right on through my coaching: it didn't matter who, even if the person was the captain.

I respected captains and was careful with them, but if they're not playing well they have to take it, the same as everyone else. They're just a player, they are no different; they can add value, but we all add value. I do believe, and Leigh Gibbs always says this, that you're all leaders in different ways on the field, but it is those people working together that lead the unit; no single leader can do it by themselves.

No one in the team, I hope, felt like they were being discarded like an old sock. My early years of coaching taught me that with 10 players you really had to keep all 10 onside so that you could play them. In those days a World Championships, say Glasgow in 1987, was 11 games in 12 days, so you had to use everybody. We had one player who injured her knee in the first game and it was serious. I played her for half a game against Scotland so she could then say she had played at the World Championships, but then she became one player I didn't have for the remainder of the tournament. Those are the things that can happen to you. You have to run the total race; that was always my phrase.

Leadership is useful, but it's not the only thing. People believing they are valued and feeling they are a part of a unit is so important in a team game. To put it another way: if you had a player who wasn't coping well on the day, and the team knew this, I would take them off because everyone else is using energy to cover for them. They look okay and the game looks okay, but why can't we find the wing attack? Why isn't she there when somebody needs her and they have to re-offer and re-pass and do something? If people know that, they work harder for that place and they honour the place. The team leader can say 'well done' later on. I must admit I was a bit sparse with praise. You are always going forward; if you're not going forward you are yesterday's player! Enjoy it, dine out on it, and I'm not saying don't do that, but I would ask them after a game, 'Are we that good or are they that bad? We won that one by 10, so let's face it they were pretty ordinary. How could we do better against a better side?'

We had a great coach in 1960 and 1963: Dixie Cockerton. She was the coach of the first seven-a-side team. She had been a player in the 1948 series against Australia in New Zealand, and she was a teacher. I would have jumped up and grabbed the moon for her because she gave you the opportunities — that was really important. I was very fortunate because the three of us — Dixie, Pam Smith (captain) and I (vice-captain) — talked about the players that we were going to play. The most exciting thing was that at the 1963 World Tournament they brought in guarding the shot; you couldn't guard the shot before that. I was enthusiastic about this as it was easier to intercept, and you could read play (where people wanted to pass the ball) from their bodies, and that came from my basketball background. That's what I loved about being vice-captain and being part of the decision-making.

When I was coach, I started off a bit mean. I had a great belief that the coach never discovers the player; they only help them discover themselves, and that was always my philosophy. In my own playing days, basketball coaches were telling you exactly what they thought you should do because there were a lot more plays and moves, and there was a degree of difficulty for the players to understand them. Yet in netball, the old dears were saying 'oh, you're doing well, dear' and it used to really get up my nose because a woman's timespan at the top of her sports career is very limited. You want to know how to get better, how to improve, so you need to say it as it is. Being exposed to different coaches while playing basketball helped form my own coaching style.

I believed that you make a 'thinking player'. I used to divide the court into groups — the attackers, middies and defence ends — and they would all have their product, and we would have a game plan for each. They had to be part of that game plan, and if it wasn't working, they had a fall-back position. Then if you work at it in training and keep repeating the stuff, they'll make decisions all the time so that when opportunities aren't coming and they're not as good as they could be, they're thinking on their feet. The players have to think how to be different and how to pinpoint problems. If a coach has a philosophy and looks at the game and sees the whole picture from the outside, and the player feels the game from the inside, when you put the two things together you really have got quite an exceptional feel for that end result. It is the combination of both perspectives that is the ultimate way to improve.

Everyone comes with skills, but not all of them are going to be as brilliant as you want them to be. So the art of coaching is to use or tweak what they've got for the whole result on court. In those early years through to 1987 I did the fitness for the team. I didn't have a trainer. I didn't have any support staff until we got a physio in 1987. When you put in the work and are at peace with yourself, the most important thing for me is that you care for each other's skills. That means I can give you a pass when you've got that horrible person defending you aggressively. When I make you look good, we're all good. So you care, and when you do that you are thinking deeper into the game and the skills, and you've practised it. I am a great believer that you can do thousands of warm fuzzy drills and look brilliant, but at the end of the day the decisions have to be made on court and under pressure where you are stretched, and it shows your Achilles heel; when you're strecthed you're only as good as your basic skills. You don't have to go and say 'that was great', you don't have to high-five each other, we haven't got time.

The greater the challenge, the greater the rewards, so you've got to train players to be whole people who feel good in their own skin. It doesn't matter if they can't shoot or defend or turn as well as somebody else, they have a job to do. When the team has put in the work, is at peace with itself and cares for each other's skills, they are linked by an invisible thread and only then are they a great team.

> I had to grow some players quickly and I was mean to those players; I really gave them a hard time, there's no doubt about it. I nearly killed them.

When I was coach I would have an 'old guard' to help lead the team. A lot of those players were great women. (I had some people in that team for nine years and they didn't get paid. None of us did; I never got paid, even to this day, but I don't care, that was never the thing — it was enjoyable. You had to be using your brain against the opposition; that's the fun of it.) I needed to know how they felt on court; in my playing days I believed that was very important. Dixie Cockerton never wanted to listen to what you felt on court. For the World Championships in 1987 I had an old guard of about three, and perhaps another one with an opinion, that I would bring in occasionally. They were people from different areas of court and I would get their feelings on how they felt their product was going and their opportunities to change. You had your piece of product on court, then you had a fall-back position if that wasn't going so well. If you coach your players to read play, then they're not coming over to you at quarter-time or half-time looking at you to solve the problem; they know that we're going to solve it all together.

Before the World Championships in 1987, I did an interesting thing that helped us win in Glasgow. (No one got within 10 points of us.) I sat everyone down when we got to England and I made them give away their secrets. I would make the defence sit down and say what they hated being done to them; they told everyone, they told the shooters, and the shooters said what they hated being done to them. So they were helping the defence, and Leigh Gibbs said, 'All hell will break loose when we go back to New Zealand because we're giving away our trade secrets.' And they were; but it made people such as Tracey Earl grow up more quickly. For example, in defence Waimarama Taumaunu was aggressive and on their body, and intimidating all the time, having a presence, and she told them the things she hated done to her. I had Tracey, who was reasonably new in shooting. I also had some of the old guard, such as Margaret Forsyth and Margharet Matenga, who were the best shooters in the world for a long time. But they were becoming predictable, and I knew that I shouldn't play them together, because people knew what they were going to do. So they had to change. An international player who becomes predictable has a limited future.

We did fitness. They were a dedicated group and they knew what they wanted to do. We would have an hour of fitness, which was mostly netball-related skills, quick work, sharp and sweaty. I was not having to growl, because there was a pecking order there in which the older players kept the younger ones on task; they believed in the philosophy, they became leaders, and the others followed. Wai said years later, 'No one's a leader unless someone wants to follow them.' One of the most exciting things for me is how many of those girls have stayed in the game and coached.

As coach, every year I had to go to the New Zealand Netball Council meeting to get the job. There were delegates from 48 associations and there was a vote held. At my first World Tournament as coach in 1975, the New Zealand team lost to England by one, drew with Australia and came third. I thought, that's it: I'm gone!

But I had got to the stage where I thought, I'm growing people, I'm developing people, I'm coaching, and I've got this philosophy because I believe the skills of the game should win. No matter what you say, no matter how someone needles you or does nasty things to you, the moment you retaliate, your own game is gone. Before the final against Trinidad and Tobago in 1979, I said to the team, if we can't play skills in this game I don't want to be in this game, because we were getting nasty things done to us all the time. You've got to have that armadillo shell, but you've also got to have a philosophy that drives you, and that you own. I would tell my players, the moment I stop learning, give up, guys, because you're teaching me as well; we're all in it together and that's the fun of it.

GD

One of the biggest challenges for me as a coach was after the World Championships win in 1987. I had a great team that was really united. They were amazing because they knew what they wanted, and several of them had been at the 1983 World Championships when we didn't handle the final very well. When I sat on the sideline of that tournament in 1987, I'd been coaching the New Zealand team since 1974, and for the first time I almost saw the work ahead to develop a new team, as three or four of them were going to retire. So when I came back to New Zealand there was a new group of players going to come into the national team. It was going to be very difficult for the next coach because Trinidad and Tobago, who came second [at the World Championships], were the team that was going to tour New Zealand the next year. I thought if the new coach got out there and Trinidad beat New Zealand — which they'd never done — the public would never forgive her. She'd have the critics on her shoelaces. So I thought I would stay on for that year, as I could afford to lose. However, I had to grow some players quickly and I was mean to those players; I really gave them a hard time, there's no doubt about it. I nearly killed them. We won the first game, but lost the second, in Palmerston North; and then in Christchurch Sandy Edge ruptured her Achilles, although we went on to win that game, and the series. After we lost in Palmerston North reporters approached with a mic and mentioned it being 'the first time you've ever lost to Trinidad and Tobago'. I replied, 'Well, that's one record we don't have to worry about any more, isn't it?'

Another challenging time was in 1986, the year before those World Championships. Waimarama had a problem with injuries, Margaret Forsyth did her knee, and I was struggling. We were playing Australia and Jamaica in what we called a Tri-Series, with two shorter games in one night. You would get Jamaica and you'd be fresh, and then one team had to go back and play Australia later — so you were tired and Australia were fresh. We had a bit of a mountain to climb, but they were only 40-minute games. The girls came into the dressing room after we had lost to Australia in the second game of the night and threw the gear down and wallowed in self-pity. I just turned around and said to them, 'I'm not upset with losing, I'm upset about your attitude and failing to learn from the loss. I can't be losing unless we're going to learn from it! If you start being emotionally involved, you're down the tube, you just can't do it, not if you want to go on. It's good if you want to go down the gurgler . . .' I remember it so well. In the next game we beat Australia — and we won the series, as it happened — but it was pretty close.

At half-time, no captain would be involved; only me. I would sit them down, put the shooters together, middies together, defence together. I'd get feedback from the old guards and I would give them my point of view. You don't want to bite the heads off chickens; you're not motivating people, but you're giving them facts and they've got to be workable. They're only going to listen to so much, otherwise it goes over their heads. That's why I coached them at training like that, too, because they had to understand what my terminology meant.

I also believe fitness is key, because then you're not worried about your own body dragging in the ground, you're thinking in the last quarter of the game, and you're having fun because the other team is struggling. So I wanted my players training under stress, and then they become a player with a repertoire.

I took a New Zealand Under 24 team to Australia in 1973. Australia were really cross with Netball New Zealand, as they wanted the New Zealand team, but the New Zealand board felt that there were some players who probably wouldn't have made the next World Championships in 1975, and they wanted to invest some money in the Under 24 team, which was quite a clever plan. However, Australia gave us a tough time; we played no test matches, but about 40 games in three weeks (some of them were shorter games in tournament play). It was a baptism by fire for me as coach, and also for the players who had never had to train very hard, but I knew what was ahead of us. I was a bit mean because I believed you had to be fit, still thinking at the end of the game, when the other players' guts are dragging on the ground. You can't say 'we should have trained better' because who really wants to hear that?

Also, we were billeted, which meant that you weren't able to just chill out and get away from people; you had to be socially inclined. That Under 24 tour set me up as being a bit difficult to get along with if you weren't fit or prepared to train. Coaching the Under 24s did a lot to form my reputation going forward. They had to be fit because I was going to kill them at training if they weren't. I communicated this to them all and sent out basic activities they were to do on their own. They could play other sports; but they had to be fit. There was no fitness advice from anyone else.

I would churn them a little bit on court at trainings. I would tell the defences what the attacks wanted to do, we'd tell the attacks what the defences wanted to do. That was fun because they had to think how to get around it. So you're giving them problems all the time; that's the challenge.

Then saying to the defence, you came out of that pretty well, and you attackers need to sharpen up a bit more.

When I took over the Wellington Shakers in 2000, it was a mixed culture in terms of the players. I coached Irene van Dyk the first year she came to New Zealand. Irene was an amazing person and I admired her as a player, for her courage and work ethic to lift the standard of her game. She had been a top player for South Africa and had to relearn the game for the New Zealand style of play. Our netball philosophy was to grow players for somebody else to use, for example Anna Scarlett [later Harrison]. We're custodians of the young. They've got to believe they can go there; they've got to own it. They've got to look in the mirror at the end of the day and ask, 'Did I sweat, did I do a good job? Did I care for that team?'

The court is just a chessboard: the players are chess pieces out there and it's how you move the chess pieces about. If a coach is cunning enough and looks after the skills of each piece, they can do okay, although it helps if you have a couple of shooters, in netball particularly. In the end, I found with my New Zealand team that I survived only with the philosophy of a mixture of youth and experience, and with a total team defence.

Not everybody loves the coach . . . There's probably always someone who feels they can play better than someone else. I don't think there were any players on the fringe, but there may have been players who felt as if they had a different opportunity and should have had more time on court, and yet I believed the opportunity was theirs. Life favours the opportunist who is prepared to work. There's never going to be a clap of thunder over you on the day and you're going to be brilliant, unless you've put in the work. It just doesn't happen, and that's the way I probably used to coach. I don't believe a coach can ever be mates with the players. There has to be a certain respect. The decisions I made were hard, but they were made for the team. If you train better, you play better, and I'll look after you; you'll be on, but only if you're prepared to do that sweating away. I believed training was 'quality sweat', because any hick can train. As a coach, time is the most precious commodity you have.

When Tracey Fear was in the New Zealand team for the first time it was during a series against England. She was nervous at training, when we were practising throw-ins from the baseline. She was busy looking around everywhere and kept putting her foot on the line, which isn't allowed, and so after about the second time (and they all I knew I was getting a bit tense), I went up to Tracey and said, 'If you put your foot on that line again

I am going to spit on your foot.' They all cracked up and I still get that story today. It cured her: she got over it and I got over it.

I hold a medallion around my neck, a gold disc given to me by the 1978 team. At our first training session together after the team was picked, they were terrible. They were emotionally tired after playing in a national tournament for a week. Their friends hadn't got in the New Zealand team and they were in, and they felt bad about it. And I said, 'You're a disaster area. Go back to the motel; I don't want to see you until tomorrow.' As the van was driving along, somebody put their hand up to their mouth as if speaking into a microphone, and said, 'The coach is not happy! This team has more work to do.' They gave me the disc with 'Disaster area '78' on one side and 'I'm not happy' on the other and I still wear it as a laugh today.

Emphasis on winning

I call it success; I don't call it winning or losing. Any player on the field who is only interested in winning and losing is going to be in big trouble because they get caught up and they don't make good decisions. If you have that piece of court that you are thinking into and improving all the time, then you are successful, and when you look at the board at the end of the game you will be ahead. I see people, even today, looking up at the scoreboard, and okay, they sometimes have to because of opportunities for shooting and time pressure; but basically I was not a fan. I never really wanted to *win* a game, but in order to be successful that product on court had to be growing. It may have meant not being totally successful on the day, but if it was growing it meant being much better tomorrow. Anyone can win a game; it's constantly winning that's hard. You've got to keep the players' focus on getting better all the time: saying, are we happy with what we're doing out there? After a game I'd have the defences talk about the shooters, asking, could they do better? Did they do well? That way it's constructive criticism, and you're growing.

The 1987 team that won the World Championships in Scotland really was a marvellous team. I spoke at an Auckland dinner before we left and I said, this team knows where it wants to be. If they get second or third at the World Champs the other teams have to be pretty good. Five of them had been at the last World Championships in Singapore, and they didn't want to be second to Australia again. [They had lost 42–47 in the final.] It was just a couple of little things and I blame myself. There were no subs; I should

The 1987 New Zealand netball team, coached by Lois Muir (second from right). *Netball New Zealand*

have switched a couple of players, but I hadn't practised it and I didn't want to do it because one player would have felt that they had failed and the other one was struggling. Coaches do these silly things. I throttled the weeds in the garden for a month afterwards thinking about it. So, you see, you're not always an opportunist at the right time.

It's different across the Tasman. At the first World Tournament in 1963, the Australians were pretty good. [Late in the match against Australia, who went on to win 37–36] the ball was at our forward end and it was going to go out; one of the Australians pushed it and that ball ran away (there were no ball girls then). We would have drawn level if we'd got it more quickly and thrown it in at the attack end. I'll never forget that. I have a saying, 'there's nothing worse than an Australian playing well and knowing it': when they jump all over each other and hug each other, you never forget it, so that was my feeling right from the word go in 1963. I did have a bit of an obsession with the Australians; over those years we did pretty well matching them and finding little chinks in their armour, but they can play well and they can be sneaky.

In the early years the foundation of netball was in schools, and that's still the case today. Netball New Zealand has set a strong development plan in place: secondary school competitions, talent selected for training, games against Australia. The five zone franchises have a second-tier Beko Netball League which gives up-and-coming players opportunities for court time. The coaches are under pressure to win and it's a great feeding group for top teams. The TV exposure pushes players to succeed. However, there is still a great need for coaches at all levels in the game.

The Aussies are more aggressive from age grades right through. Over here, young people aren't ready for a selection at that age. Also in New Zealand teams, our players tend to have babies earlier. Australians don't: they're focused solely on their careers. They're going to be 30-something before they're thinking of having kids, and then they still play. Some of our players have kids at 20.

The opportunities are there, but we need to look a little bit more at helping the tall timber. If they play anywhere near a netball court, some teacher or some mother sticks them at one end of the court and they're there for life. But they need to learn the motor skills and they need to have fun. Basketball needs to do the same. Women's basketball is pretty pathetic, too. We need to look after those tall kids when they're young.

You've got to have a squad that you can really lift, and we also need to see coaches making opportunities. A lot of coaches think, 'If we go a couple of places up this year we're fine,' but they need to look at their chessboard and see the opportunities to be successful. I want to get rid of that word 'winning', but they need to be successful so that they are growing in order to have the right score at the end of the game. Players don't do that; they are happy to sit there. It's really hard because no one wants to coach: when a team wins it's a great team, but when a team loses it's a lousy coach. Look at any sport! It's worse coaching young ones, as you have to deal with the parents, who are going crook because their kids aren't getting on.

Environmental factors

Fast5 [five-a-side netball] is great entertainment and we've trialled a two-point shot now. Australia are pushing for that, but I'm a bit resistant because I do believe that the Australians have pinched quite a lot of our game. They've gone to two-handed passes, but they run all the time, and we've picked that up and are now running all the time. Netball is like soccer and hockey were in my early days; I used to follow them because we're very similar. The play away from the ball is so important to make space, so over time New Zealand has lost that a lot more than Australia. I'm not talking about being on defence. We've got people out there saying they're going to set up a zone, but they don't know a zone from a raspberry. If they're standing in a piece of court they think they're zoning; but to zone you've got to be totally aware of who's in your area and what the structure of it is and who's pushing and who's pulling. We really need to get back to some of our core play.

I'll go back further, to Michael Jordan and the Chicago Bulls. They were a great side that played a team game. They had structures: triangles on attack, quads on defence, backdoor posts and screens, all that marvellous basketball. Three-point shots come in, some little fart comes down, shoots three-pointers and he's a god. Now the game's got boring because this has taken over and we've lost half of the skills, three-quarters of the play. I worry that without a lot of thought into the two-point shot it changes the defence's game as well.

Professionalism has changed things. In my coaching days, it was using what you had, and I believe it's the same in life: you can't go out and buy your groceries if you haven't the money. So you improvise, you have more vegetables and less processed food. I do feel we have to teach the players who are being paid. Now they're getting funding for your entertainment. Do they earn their keep? Do they train enough? They think they do, they think they're at their peak; but their coaches don't push them enough, and they're happy there. We've got young people who are prepared to sit on the sideline, take that money and not get on the court. Well, those people worry me: if I were a coach today I wouldn't be picking them in any team. That person would do better going to a less successful team and making mistakes, to see if she wants to develop a future. Why haven't we got that philosophy? Because they're happy to be cushy, and the coach doesn't push them. They're hardly going to get on! One top player sat for three years on a team's benches and when she came on and the announcer said, 'Isn't she playing well,' I felt like spitting. She'd taken the money and done minimal training and been happy. She could have gone to another franchise and probably got lots of court time and been a New Zealand player. The culture since then has changed. It is now very rewarding as more young players are getting opportunities on court at the top level, enabling them to grow their game.

It's such a contrast to those early days. In 1974, for instance, when we travelled to England, we were there for six weeks, billeted the whole time, and not getting decent food: the meat looked like chewed-up mince and the vegetables were soggy. Our hosts were nice, but they hadn't a lot of money and life was not easy. Later on, when we were there for the World Championships in 1987, we stayed in a university hostel. The 1987 team manager spent hundreds of pounds for us to take the Tube and then catch the train to games. We did a bit of training at Crystal Palace and played some games there, but it cost us money. We never had our own bus, we were travelling on public transport. It was pretty ordinary, but we'd have fun competitions. We'd be on the Underground, and the first team member to meet someone from New Zealand would get a chocolate fish; a girl came up and spoke to me, and I said, 'You come from south of Balclutha because you roll your Rs' — she was saying 'worrrk' and 'girrrl'. Everyone cracked up afterwards.

GD

As far as media were concerned, I had to sell our own game. If television wanted to come to a practice, we usually got people who were left over from rugby or some other sport and got netball as a booby prize. They didn't know a great deal about the game. I said to the players, the more we talk to them, the more we tell them, the more they know the game, the better we are in the end. It's like caring for each other's skills, really, and I reckon I educated thousands of people over those years via the media. I worked overtime to be good with the media.

There was one reporter in Christchurch that leaked a team I'd embargoed because I was making an unexpected change. He wrote about it in the paper before we played Trinidad and Tobago. The next day at the media interview, I said, 'I will speak to that gentleman later, not here,' and he was livid. I was near the end of my tether, so he could write what he liked about me. But everyone was usually good, and if there was going to be a story or somebody was injured, I would just say, 'Give me a bit of time, and you will be the first to know,' because readers were interested.

What got me, though, was the Press Association before one of the tours. We were training at Crystal Palace and a reporter came along to look at the games. And he said, 'I've come to write up for the Press Association to send a report back to New Zealand. Tell me, that one with the "C" on: is she the captain?' You felt like crying, but you're not going to. You've just got to love them, because he's going to write something about you to send home.

So we were just doing our thing, and the players became household names because they started to get on TV. We played a county team in England that came out in a uniform which some guy had said looked like the goddess Diana — golden apples and silky frock things with splits up the side — and our lot came out in their white tops with black skirts, no make-up, and they beat them, big time. You don't have to take your clothes off and you don't have to show your body to play a game, do you? You were there to apply your skills; that was the focus.

Also, I had to do all the videos. When we toured, I brought a little machine that gave me a video player with a screen in my room. I would take videos of our team and the opposition, then edit them and give them to the players to look at. It's much better now of course, and that's really important. A lot of the records, like the turnovers and rebounds, are noted by people looking at the game, but they don't see the passer giving a crappy pass if somebody drops it. They see an end result. That's why some of those stats are not the be-all and end-all.

GD

I was on the board of Netball New Zealand when we first got Milo sponsorship and we all jumped around the board table. We thought it was marvellous. Once we moved to playing indoors, and we had spectators sitting down, that's when the sponsors became interested and people started to lend women's sports a bit of support. But I also believed that you didn't get the support simply because you were a woman. In those days hockey was crying poverty, but, as I said to our people, you're selling a product; it has to be good and you need to give these people the mileage — you don't get sponsorship and just walk away. It's a learning experience, and you have to deliver. Netball did that, really. Australia's still smarting to this day that we have so much interest in sponsors; but sponsors want you to win. If you keep them involved and they see growth in young people and good young women coming forward, it's great. Women in America now, in basketball and other sports, are getting far more recognition and sponsorship than they did 10 years ago. So we've been really lucky, but we've worked for it.

Margi Matenga was unusual in that she was Rarotongan and quite young. She came to New Zealand to play tennis, actually, and then the tennis people forgot to pick her up, but she had played netball back home, so she got into netball. Margi got in there a bit earlier. Rita Fatialofa had been in an age-group New Zealand team with another coach. Lyn Gunson used to say, you need a year of Lois to get used to her and what she's going to say (that is, my phrases and things). Rita came into the side and she had tremendous skills, although she had a couple of little faults that were going to cost us. She was shy and quiet, but she got in with a group and gradually she came out of her shell, and she was okay because she knew people in the group and she was always friendly with Wai. At the end of the tour, she said thank you for saying it as it is. Her other coaches had told her she was doing well, but now she really felt that she was doing well, she had grown. She now was ready on her terms and never looked back. One of the most underrated players in the country, that girl. Marvellous. A heart as big as a horse; great opportunist.

One of the great things in your life is growing whole people, not just for netball but for life. That is most rewarding to me.

LYN GUNSON

Lyn Gunson's playing career in the New Zealand netball team spanned 1974–85, with 70 caps. This was a transition period for the national team, with the sport moving towards a different era. In her first year, she became captain, taking over from an injured Shirley Langrope for much of the 1974 campaign in England. No test matches were played by New Zealand in 1976 and 1977. The captaincy became permanent in 1978, and Gunson held the position until her retirement in 1985.

Gunson led the Silver Ferns to a three-way share of the 1979 Netball World Cup title, with Australia and hosts, Trinidad and Tobago. She also competed at the Netball World Cup in Singapore in 1983, where the Silver Ferns were runners-up after a five-goal loss to Australia. She won a gold medal at the 1985 World Games in London, with a 39–37 win over Australia, and completed the double by achieving the same result four years later as coach of the Silver Ferns in Karlsruhe, Germany. On both occasions, New Zealand beat Australia in the final. Catering for non-Olympic sports, the World Games have been held every four years since their inception in 1981. They have included netball three times (1985, 1989 and 1993).

Gunson was the fifth Silver Ferns coach. She was appointed in 1989, just four years after playing in her last international. As her coaching biography by Netball New Zealand notes, 'she made an outstanding start to her international coaching career', winning eight from eight in 1989, including guiding the Silver Ferns 'to a rare 3–0 home series sweep against Australia'.[9] She was the Coach/Administrator of the Year at the 1989 New Zealand Sportsman of the Year awards, when the Silver Ferns won the Team of the Year award. At the 1991 Netball World Cup in Sydney, the Ferns suffered a dramatic one-goal loss to Australia in the final. At the time, this was described as the 'greatest netball match ever'.[10] Lyn Gunson's Silver Ferns coaching career ended in 1993 after the

Silver Ferns were defeated 62–36 by Australia in the final of the World Games.

Lyn recalls her pride in being selected for the Silver Ferns. Having achieved her goal of making the team, she went on to become a part of its history, and helped to shape the modern game of netball. For instance, she stressed the role of coaches and managers in determining the culture of the team and how important it was that they were included. The silver fern as a symbol was considered even more special to Lyn because at that time it was not available to the general public to buy as merchandise, so only those in the netball team were able to wear it on their uniform. Lyn describes how a professional attitude prevailed, in that everyone was expected to train very hard and to measure up. A collective approach towards leadership was evident in the team.

New Zealand captain and centre Lyn Gunson and Wellington player Margaret Compton, 1978. *Stuff Limited*

The team is everybody with a common purpose, and everybody puts their shoulder to the wheel.

A New Zealand netball 'goodwill' team of the best players from national trials the previous year was created for a tour to the Pacific Islands in 1972. The team was named after trials in Hamilton, following the national tournament, which consisted of New Zealand provincial teams. I found out by accident that I had been selected. After the trials, we had stopped off at a café at Te Kauwhata on our way home to Whangārei. My mother heard my surname on the radio; it was one of those little round radios sitting on the table. I was a 16-year-old schoolgirl. It seemed pretty unreal. I was very sore at the time; I could hardly get out of the car because I'd played for two days and I had never done that before. I was so tired that it did not register for a while. Mum leapt up when she heard my name. She wasn't sure what it was about; she just heard my name, and, as it turned out, they were announcing the New Zealand team on the radio. What did it mean to me, making the team? I had tried for something and I was successful so I felt positive about that. I was also partially relieved. People around me were getting excited, but it didn't really sink in until later. Knowledge of the New Zealand team was limited as there was little media coverage or communication across the country about the sport.

Team culture

When you are leading a national team like that, the culture is a product of the people in the team. We tried to make sure that people respected each other because we used to have five or six nationalities in the

New Zealand team. Netball is one of the most multicultural sports in New Zealand, so you always had to respect other people. There was good communication between the coach and the players, and we had brilliant managers. One of the key things in New Zealand netball has always been very, very good managers, and they had a significant part to play in establishing and maintaining the culture of the team. They helped drive what the coach wanted. We had managers who were highly organised and very able to do the international PR exchanges. When I first started we were billeted (hosted) in private houses. Our managers made it clear how we were expected to behave as New Zealanders representing our country. I would be interested to know what the players thought about this because I was always in a leadership role, so I was never in the 'back of the bus'. I can only ever remember one or two incidents of people not getting on for various reasons, but it was fleeting. It wasn't an ongoing drama and there was always very respectful behaviour between people. The administrators were very fine people who had strong values. It went right through the game.

There was no induction, but there was a set of behaviours that people were very clear about. We had senior players model those behaviours. People coming into the team soon knew how they were going to operate in terms of those protocols and behaviours. Quite a few expectations were passed down in story form. Storytelling was very strong. Everybody had responsibilities, and they were expected to do them well. There would be a story about what would happen if they didn't get it right, because somebody would not have come up to scratch at some time previously. This reinforced how to do it correctly; so it's a form of induction, along with guidance from the manager, coaches and senior players.

At the time I was playing there was little media coverage. Once we had television, people could then put names to faces. I played my first national tournament as a 15-year-old and I had absolutely no idea if I was playing against the New Zealand captain or any other New Zealand player, because there was nothing visual about them in the media.

A Silver Fern is what New Zealand netball players aspire to be, but we weren't called the Silver Ferns when I was playing. The name has made a massive impact. The silver fern was significant, probably more so than I suspect it is for some people today, because you couldn't get Silver Ferns' gear. There was no merchandise, and the silver fern wasn't on anything other than our national playing kits. We were quite proud of that because of the performance of previous people in the team, but also in the kind of people that they were.

I don't remember anything specifically set up that became a ritual. We had strict training times; you knew you had to rest, you knew you couldn't go shopping. The youngest person had to look after the balls, and you never, ever forgot to take the balls to practice. It was just something that you got handed when you started. People also had individual rituals or superstitions, and they would follow those very specifically. Jobs were also allocated when a new team was formed: ice, travel luggage and other support jobs were often taught to the new players by the older players, but the managers were also exceptionally good at allocating responsibilities.

There were very strong values of treating people with respect, being honest about what you were doing, taking responsibility and celebrating difference. These values were probably not discussed in a formal setting, but the coach was very clear about what she expected and the values we held. There was a clarity of purpose and we trained hard and worked hard. There was a professional attitude and associated approach to practice and playing. If you made the team you had to measure up, and that was made very clear by the older, more experienced players. It came partly from the coach [Lois Muir] as well, because of how she set that scene, but that was more around clarity of purpose and holding people accountable.

What I would say, is that in team sports, values cannot be imposed on members of the team. People have very strong personal values. They will tolerate the team purpose, habits and behaviours as far as their own values will go, but there may come a time when that conflicts with their personal values. Those traditions have to be negotiated, and it really depends on each person's own values and how far they will concede if they are in conflict. What it comes down to is what everybody is prepared to share and do for the collective good.

Our teams were always quite self-sufficient. What we noticed about other teams was that they seemed to need to be entertained, but our players were quite happy in each other's company. It kept them together. We also worked hard as amateurs, we only had time to be focused on performance. In those days we had full-time jobs, we were busy: we were organised, self-sufficient and needed the support of family and friends to survive.

When I was coach we set up quite a strong culture, as it is often called now — though I wouldn't use that term.

Leadership

People need to know what they're expected to do, and they've got to know how to do it. Then they've got to be able to perform under pressure. That process is led by someone or a group of people. Our teams always included those in management positions. We all worked together. You go to other countries and you'll only see the players as the 'team'. We've always had a collective approach; the team is everybody with a common purpose, and everybody is putting their shoulder to the wheel. If everybody contributes in the best way that they can as an individual, then you'll get the best performance out of each individual. But it's also up to the coach and management to get the individuals in the right position — connected and working together. It's not going to be an even push on the wheel. When you get out there on the court everybody has to be in the right position, with the right attitude and know what they're doing.

We've played in some games where that determination to achieve has been exceptionally high. I remember one test match at Wembley, where there were 40,000 to 60,000 people calling for England. We had only six fit players; the rest were seriously injured. It was the final test in a series and we were up against the wall. Of the two Margarets [Margharet Matenga and Margaret Forsyth], one had a corkscrewed knee and the other had what turned out to be a snapped Achilles tendon. They weren't coming onto the court in the foreseeable future. When New Zealand is in a situation like that — when I've been captain, anyway — there was just a quiet, ruthless determination that appeared. Another time, in Melbourne, our bus was sent away by the team we were playing, and there was no other way to get to the ground. The police allocated to our building took the starting players to the game. In both those matches, the team reacted the same way, showing ruthless determination. They did not like injustice. In both of those games the score was 20 to 4 in the first quarter and we won the games conclusively. In those situations, my approach is very analytical; I feel cold and my mind is calculating solutions. I was certainly not emotional or panicking. You approach something as though you can always solve the problem, whatever it is; New Zealanders are very good at doing that in my experience. That's one of the characteristics that gets people through, along with the clarity of what you are trying to do and how. The end result is not so important, but the focus on the process is. Once you've decided that's where you're going and the end point you want, then you spend all your time thinking about how you're going to get there.

WD

The coach would select a leader, but that had to be ratified by the New Zealand netball board. They were paramount over the coach and captain. We had the same coach [Lois Muir] for quite a long time. What they looked for when they appointed her was somebody who had been a player (though I don't think they necessarily always looked for players). They looked for someone who knew about the high-performance part of the game internationally, could get on with people and had high standards.

When I first got the call to say that I was the vice-captain, I had no idea why I had been chosen. You had to be a good player and be able to uphold that performance under pressure, without becoming ineffective. So your character would have been assessed. Your resilience was probably another factor, along with being prepared to lead by example. Also, I don't seem to panic much. I was a player who had played in a lot of positions; I was patient with people; I thought a lot about the game and could play people into the game on the court. Out on the court, I led by example as much as possible.

I became the vice-captain quite quickly. It was when we were in England on tour (that was my second tour with the New Zealand team). The captain was the only surviving member of the previous World Tournament teams. At school I had been the Head Prefect and always seemed to be made the captain of the teams that I was in, so I'd never been captained by anybody else up to this point. Then, early in that 6-week tour, the captain had a serious injury and had to stay in one place. So I captained the team all the way round England. I was 19 at the time.

I played other sports, such as athletics and tennis, but you didn't have a captain for them. It was learning by doing, really, and so I tried to lead by example, to be friendly to people, to look out for them and make sure that they were happy. I had some pretty unusual experiences being put in a captain's role without having any real support or role modelling. I had nothing to learn from.

I was captain officially from 1978 to 1985, and then for two years there was no money so we didn't go anywhere or have any tests. We played some home games as the New Zealand team and I was captain after that period as well. For those years we used to have trials, then the team would be selected and we named a team but had no games. I changed this to a squad once I became coach, which made for a lot of change for the players.

In her coaching style, Lois was fairly direct and knew what she wanted. She had played netball herself in the national team, but she'd also played basketball. She and her husband were both involved in basketball, so she had good support at home. She had some ideas around the game that were slightly different than those of a traditional netball coach. She was very competitive and determined and quite clear about who she wanted to play, how and where. We went through a few changes in the team and managed to keep the underlying structure going for quite some years. She was very strong defensively in terms of her coaching. She could be quite funny; with a turn of phrase that would lighten a serious moment, which was sometimes useful and necessary.

I'm qualified in physical education and teacher-trained and a different character from Lois. I analyse the game differently, and played in different positions from her, so I have a different perspective on the game at times.

Emphasis on winning

There's something for me beyond winning. Winning is quite limiting, really. We played a game once against Singapore and it was 118 to 12, or something like that; a world record at the time. But although we won that game, it was a terrible feeling, as we had missed 36 shots as well. You know you've done something really well when you measure it against the possibilities within the game and the sport, not what happened on the day. The opposition is simply the measure of how well you've played against the possibilities. It's a different way of looking at winning. It doesn't mean that I don't think the whole point about performance sport is that you are trying to win. It's taken you one second to reach the win and decide a result; it's more important to spend the rest of your time trying to find ways to reach the outcome, concentrating on how you're going to reach it. You can do some things that are absolutely different and never seen before on the netball court. Or perhaps you've achieved something that you set out to do; you might shoot 100 per cent in a game, but still lose the game. It

Silver Ferns captain Lyn Gunson with England Roses captain Pat Watson after their match at Milton Keynes, England, in September 1979. New Zealand won 56–41.
England Netball, photograph by Brian Worrell

would be better if you could shoot 100 per cent and win, but a real victory is that you've shot 100 per cent and you have given opportunities to play to others. You couldn't improve on that if that is your only aim, unless someone gave you more ball or you created more opportunities, which comes back to the team effort. So, there's a place that people go to when they've done something extremely well, and they know they have because they've played against an opposition that's been really good and has forced them to raise their game and achieve something special.

The win against Singapore, as a world record, stands out because I felt for the opposition; they were getting absolutely hammered by us. We were bigger and stronger, and there was nothing they could do about it. It was a horrible experience; but you can't play softer because that's disrespectful as well.

Environmental factors

The rules of the game have stayed fairly consistent over time, but the interpretations haven't. In the 1970s and 1980s, New Zealand was strongly innovative, we added different types of pass. One year we backspun passes over Australia's defence and they did not appear to know what was happening for some time. When you backspin a pass it hangs in the air, so that means the defensive timing is out. I learnt to pass with both hands, which not that many people did at the time. This also changed the timing of the game and passing opportunities.

Some of us moved positions. I went from goal defence to wing defence to centre to wing attack in the time that I played. So I had to learn a lot really quickly. Lois came in one night — we were playing England the next day — and said, 'I want you to play wing attack tomorrow.' I had never played wing attack before in my life, even at school. To be playing wing attack for the first time in the international arena is not an easy thing to do . . . so I just practised and learnt by imagining in my head all night about getting off the line.

Innovation was also applied in training. Our players didn't train in terms of general fitness and conditioning. I was a physical education trained person, so my training was pretty good as I knew what to do, but we had players in the team at this time who had never trained in the off-season. When I was a coach, I introduced the idea that we had to train all year round. I also introduced a squad system, because we were getting into a situation where we had more and more international events, such as the Milo Series, the home and away with Australia, and others. When I was playing, we played in the team that was selected from trials, but when I became coach I shifted it to selecting a squad for the year, and we would name teams that would be available to do certain events. We had more people to play against. Some of the other countries were able to come here, such Jamaica and Trinidad. More countries were starting to play the game at a significant level.

We never had any direct sponsorship for the national team in that time other than a pair of shoes and some clothing. When I was coach, I had to run all of the national work off the back of a Bendon league sponsorship for what, at the time, were called the young internationals. Even though the administration brought a Milo Series here, which we were grateful for, all that did was pay for the other team to come to New Zealand. There was no national team money. We had to be pretty creative. When I was playing for the first time, we got a bit of kit. I can remember they scoured the country for shoes to fit me at one stage. Those shoes were not made for netball! I had six blisters, one under the other, on the soles of my feet because of those shoes. They didn't fit because they couldn't find my size, so the guy just told me to wear two pairs of socks. During that time, we had two changes of administration; one change ushered in payment for some administrators. Up until then it had all been totally amateur.

We also had changes in the way the umpires were interpreting the rules. People were starting to go to Australia; Auckland had a relationship with New South Wales, Christchurch had a relationship with Victoria. We had television for the first time. In fact, we had TV before anybody else, so those tapes were being sent to other parts of the world but we weren't getting anything back. Instead, everybody was looking at us. When I was coaching and playing, you were up against it all the time, because everybody knew about you but you didn't know anything about them. We liked tours because we could gauge the seniors when we watched the junior teams playing. Now they watch video footage.

For the first tour to England, in 1974, we went for six weeks and were hosted privately and moved around by car and train. Once, we went for three days without having a full meal because everybody thought the hosts had fed us. We'd get up in the morning and have breakfast, and then lunchtime was going to the practice ground of the next place. We'd get there, we'd play that night and you couldn't eat well after that because there was no food other than snacks. Then we would get to breakfast the next morning not having had proper food the night before. All those sorts of things happened because people were just beginning to learn how to tour as a group and how to host teams. There were differing expectations and habits in all the different countries. England came here, and we put them in motels or hotels. When we went back the next time, they accommodated us in hotels and stopped hosting us privately. All the things you see now started then.

WD

Pregnancy never affected the team culture, but there were two players who got pregnant on my watch. It was a difficult issue to deal with in one sense, but very easy in another. In a female game the last thing you would want is for people to get upset when players get pregnant, because that would be pretty bizarre. You'd think as a women's game we'd be more supportive than in some of the other, more male-dominated sports. There were many difficulties and that is when your own values have got to come into play. I find that if you are not clear about a strong set of values, those sorts of decisions can end up being very damaging and difficult because of the potential lack of consistency and because the decisions are not based on some strong principles and beliefs. What is fundamental to me, is that the player is more important than the game.

In one case, we found out in the middle of a series. It was the last series before an international two months later, and it was interesting for other reasons. Input came from different quarters: there were feminist perspectives, Netball New Zealand (NNZ), IFNA (International Federation of Netball Associations), friends, family and the medical profession. It was a tricky situation because we had different policies about playing while pregnant: international policy said one thing, New Zealand policy said another, and policies at a local level said something else. The feminists got involved, and their attitude was, she's not injured, so therefore it can only be a performance issue. How well is she playing? What were the medical implications? We reviewed the medical literature, but at that stage there was very little written or tested. Except that we did find out — and I knew this from a couple of other people in provincial netball — that when you're five months pregnant 30 per cent of your cardiovascular efficiency drops.

Do pregnancies affect the team culture? Probably not, because of how we set up this ethos of accepting difference. The other thing we'd always set up was to expect change, because that's normal in a performance environment. You don't spend time thinking about the past or what could or might have happened; this is a new situation, you assess it for what it is and you go forward. There was, however, a cultural difference in how the news was received in the team.

WD

Media exposure definitely had an impact on individuals in the team and the team as a whole. We had to learn very quickly not to let it affect the culture of the team. One year, after a game in Auckland, we saw a cheque being handed over to one of our players. She'd been given the MVP award, but we — the team manager, the captain and I (as coach) — didn't even know that the award was being applied to the test series! It was the first time somebody had been given money in such a way. It was money for the most valuable player of the game and there was going to be one for each of the games in the series. The marketing group hadn't told anybody in the team. It could have had a massive effect. We needed a protocol and quickly. No one in NNZ had thought about the domino effect of such a decision on the team or the players.

We sat the team down to decide what we were going to do. There were choices. Take the money as individuals or create a team fund. If you were a player who did not play a lot it was different compared to those who could create individual profiles because they always played. One or two other sports had already gone through this situation.

As soon as television and more media coverage came in we needed to develop some guidelines around what players could say about the team and others. You could talk about yourself as much as you liked when being interviewed, but you couldn't talk for the team unless specifically asked to by management. We had some guidelines and principles around how people were going to work, and they were there in order to support the culture that we had developed. That meant the people on the side line were just as valuable as the people on the court: there were 12 in this team, not seven.

After I started as the New Zealand coach in 1989, there were rule changes around substitutions. In 1990 IFNA changed the rules around team substitutions; instead of 10 on the team list it was decided that you could have 12 names available for the game. For the first time, we were able to substitute players during the game, but once a player came off they could not go back on. It was very difficult because you had to prepare for using a number of subs during the game, but also leave substitution options available for any injuries, especially for specialist positions. Allowing for injury and making tactical changes while maintaining playing and positional choices to the end of the game was complex.

IFNA moved to allow 12 players at the World Championship Rules discussion on the game. Dawn Jones, President of NNZ, was our representative at that meeting and informed me we were playing international rules as of that meeting.

I remember arriving in Australia soon after, and there are 10,000 people sitting in the Sydney stadium for our first test. Half an hour before the game the opposition's CEO comes in, calls me out of the changing room and says, Lyn, you need to take two people off the team sheet. I said, 'No I don't, because that's the current international rule.' She said, 'No it's not.' We had a complete stand-off — the threat was to call the game off. The game is to start in 30 minutes and the players are warming up in the changing room. I conceded on the basis that they confirmed the next day, which they did. They also apologised. Those are the kinds of situations you are faced with when things aren't going smoothly around you politically.

That's just one example; there were many others. You can't panic; you've got to think, and you definitely can't get emotional. Numerous other incidents occurred, because it was all new — this growing international exchange in the sport.

As far as sponsorship goes, NNZ used to levy all netball players. It was about 20 cents at the start, and then it was 50 cents. It wasn't much, but there was always a reserve pot that built up over time because of the numbers playing. In those times, there was minimal sponsorship, but people don't sponsor something they're not going to get a return on. Most of the time it was about donations or people assisting as amateurs. All of the local provincial teams would get a bit of help from Mr So-and-so's garage or whatever it was, but in terms of a national team there was no payment. I've never had to pay to go away on a tour and the host country supplied accommodation and food. There was always some money there, and it allowed us to play as the national team without it having too much of an impact on our personal finances. But that's only because netball was a very big sport. In other sports, people had to pay everything. We were very lucky in comparison.

Anne Taylor, president of Netball New Zealand from 1978 to 1987, was very active. She took the game from the amateur era through to the next point, where Dawn Jones took over in 1987. They were both exceptional as presidents. The office moved from Wellington to Auckland, where there was more contact with various commercial sectors. The introduction of the Bendon league, a national club competition, helped with the development of young players, and the Milo series brought an international team to New Zealand. That was a way of getting the New Zealand netball team regular international competition. We couldn't afford to go to these countries, but if somebody brought overseas teams to New Zealand it was highly beneficial to the game. You could get a sponsor for that, but you couldn't get a sponsor for us going the other way. Anne Taylor also got the game televised. She picked a gap in the [sports] calendar, so we would always play series around March and April, which is not the end of the season. She was really clever at getting more profile. Towards the end of her time, we started to get sponsorship with Adidas. Other sponsors came on board with kit, and personal profiles began to develop.

WD

People were acknowledged holistically. If you genuinely appreciate who somebody is, then that should incorporate an appreciation of their culture. The symbols of their ethnic origin may not be obvious, but the feeling and meaning is there. At an elite level, the focus is on the sport and achievement, but recognition of ethnicity can assist performance. Most New Zealanders are very group-oriented — we always had an easiness about the group. This harmony was unique in netball and was there for a long time. I'm not sure if it's there now. I do have feelings about when that might have changed. Certainly in the time that I was involved, people were very sensitive towards each other as human beings and very accepting of each other for the person they were.

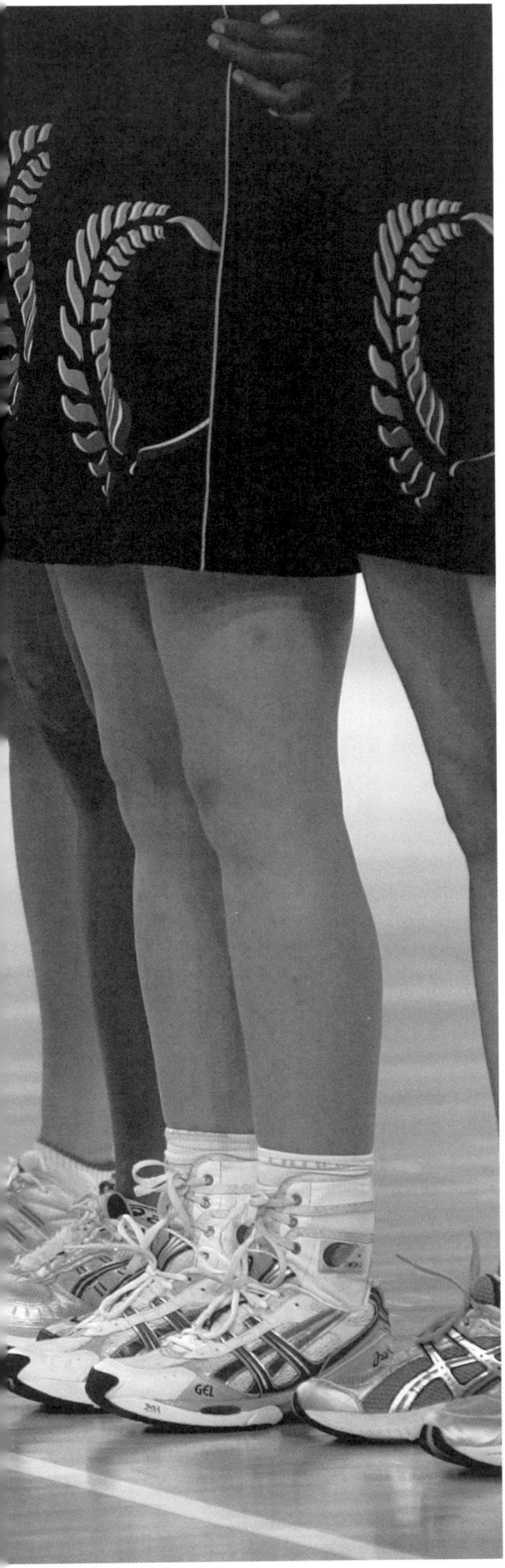

PART 3

Development, rebranding and commercialism 1988–2001

The period between 1988 and 2001 was, for the most part, a challenging era for the Silver Ferns. By the early 1990s the core of the highly successful 1980s teams had mostly retired and it took some time to develop players to replace them. Compounding these difficulties, sport itself changed significantly in this period. The government became far more actively involved in sport, via the Hillary Commission and regional sports trusts. On the one hand, this presented opportunities, such as the Prime Minister's Scholarships (which help outstanding athletes further their education while continuing in sport). On the other hand, it meant a significant reorganisation of the sports sector, with national sports organisations becoming more businesslike and corporate jargon creeping in. In response, netball had to adapt — with, for instance, the national organisation changing its name to Netball New Zealand and formally adopting the name Silver Ferns for the national team.

The 1990s saw many New Zealand team sports enter the professional era: notably rugby union, which became professional in 1995, and rugby league, which received a boost in profile when the Auckland Warriors entered the Australian rugby league competition in 1994. Netball took some important steps in this direction: first with the Bendon league and, during the 1990s, with the semi-professional National Bank Cup, which gave most participants a modest income and saw a few elite players very well rewarded.

The culture of the Silver Ferns also changed, possibly in response to these wider developments. The induction process for new players became more formalised. Later in the era, the support staff expanded to include the position of assistant coach. There were also more media obligations. As New Zealand society became more multicultural, so too did the team. There was a more prominent Māori and Pacific Island presence, and players of South African ancestry were also selected. In addition, elements of Māori culture began to be more formally reflected within the team, including visits to marae.

TABLE 4: NEW ZEALAND VS AUSTRALIA, 1988–2001*

YEAR	EVENT	NZ SCORE	AUS SCORE	WINNER
1989	Milo Series	47	46	NZL
1989	Milo Series	51	47	NZL
1989	Milo Series	49	37	NZL
1989	World Games	33	29	NZL
1990	XIV Commonwealth Games	35	53	AUS
1990	J & J Series	42	44	AUS
1990	J & J Series	57	51	NZL
1990	J & J Series	40	52	AUS
1991	8th World Championships	52	53	AUS
1992	Kleenex Cup	46	67	AUS
1992	Kleenex Cup	45	55	AUS
1992	Kleenex Cup	37	64	AUS
1993	World Games	36	62	AUS
1994	Milo Series	49	52	AUS
1994	Milo Series	44	47	AUS
1994	Milo Series	53	49	NZL
1995	9th World Championships	44	45	AUS
1996	Milo Cup	40	49	AUS
1996	Milo Cup	39	58	AUS
1996	Milo Cup	35	56	AUS
1996	Fisher & Paykel Cup	41	52	AUS
1997	Fisher & Paykel Cup	43	49	AUS
1998	Fisher & Paykel Cup	47	58	AUS
1998	Fisher & Paykel Cup	49	58	AUS
1998	Fisher & Paykel Cup	48	52	AUS
1998	XVI Commonwealth Games	39	42	AUS
1999	Fisher & Paykel Cup	60	48	NZL
1999	10th World Championships	41	42	AUS
2000	Fisher & Paykel Cup	30	53	AUS
2000	Uni-Bank Tri-Series	52	40	NZL
2001	Tri-Nations	55	40	NZL
2001	Tri-Nations	52	62	AUS
2001	Fisher & Paykel Series	47	51	AUS
2001	Fisher & Paykel Series	58	47	NZL
2001	Fisher & Paykel Series	46	50	AUS

*No games were played against Australia in 1988

LEIGH GIBBS

Leigh Gibbs was a Silver Fern for 10 years (1978–87), winning 61 test caps. She was captain when they won the World Championships in Scotland in 1987. Gibbs also coached the Silver Ferns from 1994 to 1997, in which time they played 32 tests, winning 24 and losing eight for a 75 per cent success rate.[11] She was also assistant coach from 2001 to 2007 with Ruth Aitken (née Fathers). She later coached the Mainland Tactix from 2012 to 2014, and in 2015 accepted a position with Netball Queensland as General Manager — Sports Development.

In her interview Leigh explains how team culture was considered hugely important, and she felt this was a strength of the New Zealand team. During her time as coach and assistant coach a lot of off-court work was done, alongside some more formal approaches, to help foster this team culture. Other key points she notes are the establishment of formal groups to develop leadership, and the induction process of new players in the team.

Leigh's coaching style was very much based on empowering her players to become better decision-makers and to learn to be responsible for their own development. She also encouraged them to ask questions and have open conversations. Her philosophy on leadership is that everyone has the ability to be a leader, but people have to be confident in their ability and their performance and lead by example in order to demonstrate effective leadership.

Ultimately you want to empower players to be able to be fully responsible and confident on and off the court.

When I was selected for the national team, there was no formal induction. It was 1978, and the last time the Silver Ferns (or the New Zealand netball team, as it was then known) had been picked was in 1975 for the World Tournament, so some time had elapsed. You were selected for the New Zealand trials based on performances at the national tournament the year before. From memory, around 21 players were selected to trial across two days. We were played in several positions, and at the completion of the trials we all went into a room for the team announcement. The names of the successful trialists were called out alphabetically. That process of coming together as a group for the trials, having two days of playing and then the team announced continued for most of my Silver Ferns playing career.

I came from Gisborne, a small city, where netball and hockey were the winter sport choices for girls. It was an era when there was no netball on television, so what you were exposed to was only within your immediate environment. I really didn't know many of these top netball players; nonetheless it was exciting to come together for New Zealand selection. I had spent three years in Dunedin prior to trialling, so I had met a couple of them; Lois Muir lived in Dunedin and was the incumbent New Zealand coach, and Lyn Gunson was a leader in my club. It felt like a new era because there were a lot of changes, a lot of young or new faces on the scene, so it was very, very exciting.

When the names were called out you were listening for your name alone. It wasn't until the end of the announcement that you became aware of the ones who had missed out. When my name was called I didn't want to get too excited in front of the others. As my maiden name was Mills and midway through the alphabetical list, it was hard to remember who had been selected.

With the 1978 series, though, an interesting phenomenon took place, which I do not think occurred again. I know Lois didn't enjoy the time frames, and arguably it wasn't a great way to prepare for a test series, but the team that got named stayed on together after trials. So in preparing for the trials, you had to think, if I get picked I'm going to be away for another two weeks. You thought, do I pack my bags for being away for the trials *and* test series, or do I play it safe and just pack for trials? It was weird, in that we were going to be staying on as a new group for two weeks, and then one week after that we were going to play Trinidad and Tobago.

Lois had to deal with a lot of newbies: more than half had not played for New Zealand before. The senior players at the time, who had been in the previous New Zealand team, were Lyn Gunson, Yvonne Willering, Millie Munro and Maxine Blomquist.

There was no formal induction process: you just had to get over your tired body on your own. There were no physios at the time. It was very challenging for everyone and, in particular, Lois. We were tired players who were naturally very excited to be playing for New Zealand, but equally we had had no recovery time, no ice baths, and we probably hadn't hydrated very well between our trial games.

The whole selection programme changed for the better over the time of my playing involvement. You weren't just selected on one weekend of trials; they looked at player performances on and off the court. There was feedback to players after that, too, but as I never got dropped I don't know what was done with those who missed out — whether they were given any support or feedback as a player. Towards the end of my playing career, we had a catch-up with Lois, one-on-one, prior to or during the trials, and we would talk about what she was wanting to see from us. But she never gave any hint if we were in or out at that point. It was after selection that Lois sent us her handwritten feedback from trials. There were a lot more one-on-one discussions around player development, approach of the players, and what needed to be done.

Team culture

The team culture is hugely important, and it is a strength of the Silver Ferns. When I was coach we struggled sometimes to execute consistently and under pressure, but the sort of work that we'd done with the team culture off court was really important. When I played, there wasn't too much done formally. In the 1987 team there were good people with experience and a strong sense of self, and clarity of what the team was aiming to achieve. Although there were few formal team values sessions, the way that Lois coached and communicated with us, she was able to develop this informally. The more formal approach has developed strongly, in my experience, since my move into coaching. We need to keep providing settings to develop leadership in players, both formally and informally, which has to be constantly worked on and polished. So discussions around vision would be scheduled, and we would self-evaluate and team-evaluate both on-court and off-court performances. We were subjectively evaluating, using a visual representation to brainstorm and share our thoughts.

In my first time as a coach of the Silver Ferns [1994–97], I didn't have an assistant coach, so the management team was the manager, a physio and me. In my time as a player, there had been no physio until my final two years in the team. Certainly when I was an assistant coach there was a lot more thought around an induction process that was probably handled both formally and informally through the squad camps and communication to the players.

When I was coaching, players received a handbook that covered a range of expectations in an operational sense. A lot of the other expectations were done together in a team sense, through interactive sessions and a varied range of team activities related to team values, and discussions around player responsibilities. These opportunities increased when I was Ruth Aitken's assistant coach, as the programme provided more time together as a squad or team. When I was head coach, while we did have squad camps, time together and people resources were still limited. With more time, Ruth and I focused on building a strong unit, developing our team vision and culture, which included player inductions. There was a lot of work around what it meant to be a Silver Fern, both on and off the court, from a branding and marketing viewpoint as well as being part of a team. It was a multi-pronged, holistic approach. Importantly, the players needed to understand their role in both netball in New Zealand and in the national team.

Leigh Gibbs coaches the Mainland Tactix at a team practice, 2013. *Stuff Limited*

A specific example would be around some team-building, team vision, culture and expectation discussions leading into the campaign. We also gained much from the contribution of external expertise. As an example, [mental skills coach] Gilbert Enoka and I worked together when I was head coach of the Silver Ferns. Gilbert and I were teaching colleagues at Hillmorton High School in Christchurch and shared many ideas about what made a great team. When I was coaching the Canterbury team, and with the Silver Ferns at the World Champs in 1995, Gilbert and I worked together, and he was included in team management. Leading into the 2003 World Cup campaign, Gilbert was involved again, working with Ruth, me and the players on our team vision. His approach was collaborative and was outstanding. He guided and facilitated sessions that enabled the players to develop a shared vision that really connected us as a team for what was to be a very successful campaign.

I recall that, as a team, we were trying to find something that would be unique for us, and also acknowledge where we had come from. There had been a number of heartbreaking losses to Australia by just one goal over a number of World Championships, and many of the players and team management had also experienced down-to-the-wire games in the Commonwealth Games. The team had spent a number of sessions agonising over what could be the theme for our campaign. With Gilbert's help, we established a really strong theme and symbols that we could connect to strongly both as individuals and as a team.

In that 2003 World Cup campaign, we had what we called our 'passion kete'. As a player, Belinda Colling introduced the idea that it was something that we would take away with us to the World Cup in Jamaica. There were some criteria around how many items and what you put in it, and it was to be filled with items that were special to the person. Each day, once we got to Jamaica, one person would share the items in their kete and the stories behind each item. It became a really emotional sharing time, because we each shared a part of ourselves that gave some insight into who we were. While on tour we also had what we called a daily 'morning report', where operational matters were communicated. On another campaign we shared our individual stories — where we had come from to get to be a Silver Fern.

During my time as assistant coach with Ruth, the coaching was evolving. As well as having more time with the players, we put an emphasis on team culture and developing that cohesiveness off the court, which obviously then would help on the court. That was a hallmark of Ruth's coaching and also something that I really enjoyed working through, and the players bought into it.

Leadership groups provided opportunities for the players to grow their leadership skills as well as sharing the workload across the whole team. These components demonstrated some of the changes that were taking place in the style of coaching from when I was a player.

As former teachers, Ruth and I incorporated our teaching styles into our coaching. As the Silver Ferns matured under us, so did our coaching partnership. Stronger communication through shared responsibility, and buy-in from the players, strengthened the relationships between players and team management, and contributed to our success.

We also introduced player-only meetings, where the players could come together to discuss team needs among themselves. Any feedback or queries would then be fed upwards to team management by the leadership group. When this process first started there was often quite a long list of requests and issues from the players. As time went on, the number of issues steadily reduced, signalling a strengthening sense of trust and empowerment throughout the whole team and team management. It became an amazing environment in which challenge was encouraged and embraced by all.

WD

Values among players were not formally written down, but were passed on and demonstrated. The senior players of the time, such as Lyn Gunson and Yvonne Willering, passed the values down through their actions and how they challenged you as a player. When they left the team, and I became a senior player, it was my turn. I didn't believe in a hierarchy, but there was a sense of experience in the group and a lot of mentoring that took place in an informal way. As experienced players, we took responsibility for the effort that we put out on court in games and training, including making sure we were always organised at training sessions, and demonstrating positive behaviours on and off the court. Thankfully, to my knowledge, there was never a concern around what players might do on a tour; it was all pretty innocent, really.

I remember one nightmare for Lois and Betty Steffensen, the manager at the time. We were in the middle of a home series against England and

I'm pretty sure we were staying in the same hotel as the French rugby league team. There were a whole lot of gorgeous-looking guys wandering around. I am sure Betty breathed a sigh of relief when we moved on to the next test venue! However, she didn't really have anything to worry about.

So there were no stated values that I was aware of during my playing years. However, through the leadership of the older players, team management and our own standards, the Silver Ferns generally set a high bar. The challenging thing was ensuring everyone had a clear understanding of their role, as it was all fairly informal. I can't recall any sessions on establishing the team vision, what culture meant and what being the ideal player was. However, the legacy left by former players and passed down through the teams meant a lot of different players instilled and discussed what behaviours we were looking for.

Players not getting on court was a challenge I had to deal with when I was coaching. At that time, the substitution rule only allowed up to three subs in a game, and if you came off you couldn't go back on. Players then were more accepting of not getting on court. In my early years as a provincial representative player there was no substitution rule at all, and it wasn't uncommon for players to get no court time during a tournament. To my knowledge, players mostly accepted it. Coaches rarely discussed or gave feedback on what you needed to do to get onto the court. In today's coaching environment, feedback to the player is essential and expected. Players rightfully want to know what their chances are of getting on court and what they have to do to get there. Some players actually want very detailed information and to be told what to do when out on court.

My coaching style encouraged the players to be better decision-makers, and to take responsibility for their own development, to grow their capability. If they were unsure of what we were wanting, then we encouraged a two-way conversation. But also that they have the openness to challenge and ask questions.

A coach needs to provide the 'why' and ask questions to gain better understanding and to use the values session to build the concept of the team being greater than the individual. As these are usually done earlier on in the programme, when the pressure is less, it is not until the pressure comes on that the team's values and behaviours face the true test. If everything's going smoothly, then being extra alert is important so that you can anticipate whether and where that will change.

Leadership

As coach, I always had a mind-set and overarching philosophy that everyone should be a leader at some point. Part of leadership is knowing yourself well and knowing what impact you are having on others. High-performance sport is a high-pressure environment, so you need to be confident around your own playing performance, to help others and lead by example. Having really good communication skills is vital; being that conduit between team management and people outside of the team. Within the team leadership environment, that may mean translating messages that might not otherwise be understood by your teammates, initiating and fostering discussion, and curtailing stuff quickly that perhaps is against team values. They really need maturity and support around these skills — so you need to understand where that line is, but do it in such a way that your teammates and your people are not feeling belittled.

Good leadership absolutely contributes to a winning team. Growing leadership will always be a constant because it's such a huge component of success. Also understanding that leadership has many faces; it's multi-factorial. Players understanding where they fit and knowing who they are is important and leadership helps people to grow that understanding. Good leadership is a constant, because you will have a lot of small things that will eat away at the culture.

WD

Captaincy is best suited to someone who has confidence and consistency in their performance. I was appointed captain, and also felt I was respected by, and was respectful of, both the team and Netball New Zealand. Strong communication skills clearly encompass all of that. A captain needs a very good understanding of the tactical elements and on-court ability to initiate a change-up when needed, or help someone perform. They need to be self-sufficient, self-aware and calm under pressure, and they also need to be really good communicators at all times.

As I got more experience as a captain, my confidence grew. When coaching with Ruth, we wanted more group leaders in the team and Ric Charlesworth's leaderful team concept [Ric coached the Australian women's hockey team to the gold medal in 1996 and 2000] was a concept we really endeavoured to develop.

So what are the behaviours that need to be exhibited and developed in the players? As coaches, how do we grow that in our players so that they are more confident around leadership and understand its many elements and forms?

As a captain I was self-contained. That's my definition, and to me it means that I was comfortable in myself. That is something Lois saw as an important component; and not just in a captain, but in all players. I had developed some of the elements from my teaching background, as well as skills in communication. Physical education was my teaching subject. When I was playing there were no support service personnel around the team. My experience in those aspects was helpful. I was hard-working; I have a reputation for that and I got on well with Lois. I would say we had good communication, because you can't have a coach and captain that don't. You've got to be able, as captain, to have strong connections with all of those components.

When I became coach, my reputation as a player helped and the fact that I had success with the Under 21s at World Youth Champs. Georgie Salter [née Hapuku] was co-coach with me, so that was an interesting and successful dimension.

I knew Ruth, but not overly well, before becoming her assistant coach. She'd been an opposing coach to me at national champs and the National Bank Cup. When she rang and asked if I would be her assistant, it was a very surprising but exciting conversation. Her comments, roughly from memory, were around me having had experience as a coach at World Championships, which she didn't. Some of my most enjoyable coaching experience was spent working with Ruth and coaching at those events. Things weren't always successful; in fact, there were some really challenging aspects. The pressure or expectation from media is another element. Being comfortable with the media was something I learnt on the job as captain, as there was no training provided at the time.

As captain of the Silver Ferns, I would discuss strategy with Lois. Video was just coming in as a coaching tool. We would sit through VHS tapes and look at lots of game footage. When I first came into the Silver Ferns as a young player I was scared of Lois, because it was a hugely different era. Over our time together, I became really comfortable with her, and she with me. In the 1987 World Cup campaign we would have great tactical discussions, including some with Tracey Fear, my vice-captain.

Later, as a coach, I felt my communication skills got better with experience. I also gained more trust from the players, and so better relationships grew from that. Importantly, as coaches, we have a view of what we want from the team and how we like to operate, but we must check and see if it is understood and valued by the players. This is important in a high-pressure environment where it's easy to slip back into old ways and take things for granted. I learnt to keep continually checking with the players that we were on the same page, as I could never assume anything.

There are a lot more opportunities created now for communication with our teams than there were when I was a player. In the ANZ Championship environment, having weekly catch-ups with the support staff was important. We would check in with players on how we were tracking in the programme. Were we achieving the intensity we wanted, and were all the on- and off-court elements happening as they should? Were there any concerns? This would also include the players, with different pairings coming in to each meeting, not just captain and vice-captain: we included the whole playing group with support staff and team management. We went through each player one by one. So a lot more time was spent on checking communication and understandings and assessing where people were at. That didn't happen when I was playing.

When we were successful as a team when I was playing, there were a couple of players that may not have been on the same page, but the bulk of the team were. Their experience and motivations weren't quite the same as the older players' in the group. That is probably pretty common because young players are still learning. As a coach, my first head coaching issues were down to communication — sometimes mine. And I didn't handle some personalities as well as I could have done.

As captain, my approach was to lead by example in terms of effort and commitment on court. I had a passion for the game and for the position I held, and I hope that I demonstrated those qualities. Then, as a coach, certainly working with Ruth, it became clear that we as leaders were going to have open communication with the players, but also that on some decisions we needed to make tough calls.

It is important to show a united front in all aspects of management. We needed to have one view, for consistency's sake, even if some discussion was needed to reach that point. As a coach, you must also say what you mean and mean what you say. You can't say one thing then mean something else. The other important change in the coaching environment

Leigh Gibbs talking with the players of Mainland Tactix, 2012. Deciding on the level of instruction during game breaks is part of the art of coaching. *Michael Bradley*

was bringing in different voices; using specialist coaches was a really positive move.

I endeavour to continue to keep the same philosophies, but what I found challenging [about coaching in the ANZ Championship] was the player payment element of it. Players were no longer playing at an ANZ level because they were loyal to a particular geographical team, space and place. Having clarity around their purpose — why they were there — was an important part of the team environment. What's their motivation and their reason for playing?

The ANZ environment had different challenges to the Silver Ferns environment. At ANZ level the season went for six months of the year versus a Silver Ferns campaign that might consist of several training camps over a couple of days and then a test series. While the outcomes were higher, such as winning a test series or a World Cup, it was within a very short, intensive time frame.

Coaching is really like a continuum: when the pressure is high during a game, you might need to give players more direct instruction at the brief game breaks than you would at training. Ultimately, you want to give players empowerment and confidence to take full authority. The art of coaching is learning how to do that — and it comes more easily when you're doing it regularly. Ultimately, I love that element of coaching, and a really good example was towards the end of my stint with Ruth. Midway through the final game of the World Cup against Australia we had a player sent off court, Temepara Clark [née George]. We had prepared the team really well with a lot of 'what if' scenarios, one of them being just this. When it actually happened, the players took control. As Temepara was our centre, we needed to shift someone into her position. The players knew and made the required changes, with Lesley Rumball [née Nicol] moving from wing defence into centre. To me that was the ultimate. We had done our job because at the height of the World Championship final, in a crucial part of the game, the coaching team didn't have to do anything; it was all taken care of by the players. That, for me, was absolute proof that we'd done our job.

Emphasis on winning

To me, winning has many dimensions; it is not just about the score. Do players come back, do they stay in the game, and do they continue to contribute? For a coach, winning is when you've got a good return on all those things. If that comes with a World Cup title, that's the icing on the cake, and it will be influenced by the environment you've created.

Winning is hugely important, but I have found in my development as a coach that if you focus only on winning and forget the process, it will be to your and the team's detriment. As a player, you're not thinking about outcomes, processes and strategies. I certainly wasn't at that time. I just went out to be as prepared as possible and do the best I could, and I trusted people around me to do the same. The coaching and team management were there to support us and provide direction. Then, in the coaching space, you've got to be really well prepared, so again the focus is on the process. Winning was always there — you couldn't avoid it — but if it becomes your sole focus, you're at risk.

When I went to the Tactix — and this is still something teams are grappling with — we wanted to win, but was our understanding of the will to win bone-deep? The will to win had to be embedded in our expectations and behaviours. I was talking to [Australian ex-Diamond] Roselee Jencke recently about when she first arrived in 2010 to coach the Queensland

Firebirds, and they finished fifth. After that year, some new players from other parts of Australia came into the team whose understanding of winning was probably different. At one of their early discussions as a team, one of the players said, 'I didn't come here to come second; I'm here to win,' and that expectation became embedded in the team. At the Tactix we needed some more players to come in with that kind of game-winning approach; but that doesn't happen instantly. In the Silver Ferns you're clearly going to have that expectation because the team is used to winning. It doesn't have to be put out there loudly; there's more of an unwritten sense that when you put the silver fern on, you're expected to get over the line.

Standout games were the ones where the outcome was huge. World Championships, of course; but, interestingly, a game that stands out for a slightly different reason was the the last game in the 1986 series with Jamaica and Australia. We had lost to Australia five times. So when we beat them, it was the final game in the six-game series, and it was quite significant for me. While I wasn't on the court because I was injured, I felt that the team had overcome the disappointment of the losses as a group. We knew we weren't at our best by any means, and that win really showed us, or showed me, that it was the turning point, and clearly the following year — winning the 1987 World Championship — we built on that.

From my coaching days, an early win would have been in my first series against Australia. We won the final test and that was again on the back of several losses. So for a beginning high-performance coach, that was a real confidence boost. The World Cup win in 2003 in Jamaica provided a huge sense of relief because there had been such a history of World Cup losses to Australia by one or two goals. I can't remember what the score was but it felt like we had total control. Even when Temepara got sent off, it didn't disrupt us. It could have derailed our performance, but it didn't, so that was significant.

As a player, I particularly recall our loss to Australia in the Singapore World Champs. The World Champs was the pinnacle, and Singapore was a challenging environment because we played outdoors in the heat. Everyone was exposed to it, of course, but that loss was devastating. But it fuelled the resolve for most of that team to stay in there and change it up, and get the result we wanted at the next World Champs. Certainly, in the World Cup that I was the coach [1995], it wasn't so much the South African game but the Australia game that really disappointed me, because it was

Winning is hugely important, but I have found in my development as a coach that if you focus only on winning and forget the process, it will be to your and the team's detriment.

there for the taking. Whoever was going to lose had a lot to lose, and I found that hugely disappointing.

Then, with Ruth, it was probably the World Cup in 2007 in Auckland. It felt as though we could have done it, but we couldn't get over the line. You reflect on what you might have done differently, what could have changed the result.

It appears to be harder for Australian players to make the Diamonds, with more players vying for selection and greater competition at state level. Australian players are exposed to more competitions, more netball, so that by the time they get into the Diamonds they're more experienced than our players, with an element of hard-won confidence. Kiwis tend to be a little lacking in that as we haven't had as much tough competition to get into the Silver Ferns. So it takes some time to acquire that resolve and develop as high-performance players.

New Zealand has players with a great range of skills. Australian netball talk about a style, the Australian way, whereas New Zealand netball is not so specially defined, and I believe our approach caters for the different types of players that make up the Silver Ferns: Polynesian, Māori, European and South African. Australian defence is known for its hard one-on-one style, whereas here we are more known for the zone style of defence. We need to be able to have variety and be able to do both. So New Zealand's variety of styles takes time to gel. Australians are very clear around how they want the game played. This slight difference in approaches could affect how teams build confidence to win and grow that understanding earlier.

Environmental factors

When I was a Silver Fern, netball was starting to enjoy good television coverage, and the public awareness of the team was growing. An issue back then, which incensed several in the Silver Ferns team, was when one journalist wrote a headline-grabbing article about the team being too old (myself included), and that there needed to be changes, including Lois, who was coach at the time. That was on the back of the five losses in a row to Australia in the Tri-Series between New Zealand, Australia and Jamaica. As a player, I felt for Lois. Once netball got on television the increased coverage started to have an impact. I still recall Lois saying that you couldn't fail quietly when you were in the New Zealand team. When you wore the silver fern you were out there in the public eye and that was always a pretty tough learning environment, as a player and certainly as a coach.

When I was selected to coach the Silver Ferns it was a surprise. I enjoyed a bit of a honeymoon period, with some good results. At the World Champs in 1995, losing to South Africa in our second game of pool play meant that we faced Australia the next day. The stakes were high as whoever lost would be playing off for third place against England. What was really challenging was not only heightened interest from media, but also having to do a live interview with Paul Holmes [then host of a prime-time show on TVNZ]. It was our morning (so evening in New Zealand) and I did it by phone. He said something to the effect that because the game was played in the morning in New Zealand cars were stopped on the side of the road listening to the Australia game — and we lost. That overwhelming sense of disappointment from the nation: how did I feel about that? We were gutted.

The other challenging aspect about the loss to South Africa was that there was a planeload of supporters coming over to watch the second leg of the World Champs, and in particular hoping to see New Zealand play Australia in the final. We played England in the third/fourth play-off, so the supporters were devastated. Not only did they not see New Zealand against Australia, because they were on the plane, but they also didn't get to see the Ferns play in the World Cup final. At a supporters function a day after the game I apologised to them all publicly on behalf of the team.

The draw format was questionable. I'd watched South Africa play England in November 1994. South Africa beat England five–nil in that series, and yet South Africa was put in our pool at the World Champs. We shouldn't have lost to them, but meeting Australia the following day made it very challenging. Getting the team through that huge loss, the anger, the grieving, and then having to play Australia the next day and lose by one goal was character-building.

I was reappointed to the coaching position the year following the World Champs in 1995, and the scrutiny of my coaching increased until I was dropped as coach in 1997, two years before the 1999 World Champs. When I was appointed to the assistant coach role in 2002, with Ruth as head coach, the scrutiny continued. Initially, the media questioned whether I was actually coaching the team. This situation was highlighted in the first series we coached together in Jamaica. A photo taken at an interval in the game showed me with a group of players (the defence unit) and did not include Ruth, who was with the attacking unit. The headlines read, 'Who's really coaching this team?' Thankfully we were offshore, and there was no social media to add fuel to the fire. Ruth and Kerry Manders' [Netball New Zealand's head of communications and marketing] strong relationship meant that we could anticipate or perhaps change things up if there was any potential controversy.

There are a whole lot of other elements in play, particularly when you lose. It's all part of the environment now and just part of the skill set needed by coaches, captains and players. Media training is crucial. It's a huge element of high-performance athletes. Thankfully netball continues to present a positive image in the media, although there has been criticism for this at times. I certainly believe that Netball New Zealand and all our coaches have done really well to promote netball, themselves, captains and players in a very positive light.

Game analysis is also becoming a key part of the high-performance coaching environment. Coaches and players need to understand where that fits; what is the balance between the science and the art? In my early time as a player, it was all on-court stuff and the knowledge of the coach and the players around us that contributed to our performance, but now there are a whole lot of other elements influencing this.

There have been several changes since my day. The rules and umpire interpretations, for instance, allow the defending players to contest more. In the early days, when I was a defender, there was a sense that the rules favoured the attacking players. When the game moved indoors, that enhanced the opportunity to contest, because if there were collisions you weren't going to hurt yourself on the wooden floor versus outside on the asphalt. It enabled the players to feel that they could go for the ball. There was also the increase in speed of the ball through the court, as you weren't influenced by the weather. Shooters obviously did not have to worry about wind, rain and sun. I've played some test matches in windy conditions outdoors, which had a huge impact on the game.

There were no substitutions allowed in my early playing days. Once the seven were named, you wouldn't get on the court unless someone got injured. That has changed and the game has progressed, challenging the coaches and players to make the transition of new players coming on seamless. Much work was (and still is) needed around managing substitutions.

Off the court there's a lot more one-on-one work with players around developing their individual performance plans and understanding the preparation needed for high-performance sport. The head coach now needs to work well not only with the playing squad, but also with the bigger support services team, thus requiring greater people management skills. In my early days as a player, the team was made up of the players, coach and manager. This group grew to include a physio, then in my final year as national coach I could add an assistant coach.

So now the coach needs to be the overseer of a much wider group and programme. They need to understand all the roles and responsibilities and the impact each has. There are also a lot more tests played each year. When I first got into the Silver Ferns in 1978 they hadn't picked a team since 1975. Following a World Cup, there were no Silver Ferns selected in 1980 and 1984. This gap enabled countries to build up funds, as sponsorship was unheard of then. Sponsorship now has a huge part to play, and a good understanding of the expectations of sponsors is another requirement for high-performance coaches.

When I was a player, certainly, players trained, but the science now around strengthening and conditioning is very different. With my phys-ed background I had a bit of knowledge around what I needed to do, and was seen as someone who worked hard on my fitness. I saw it as a responsibility to my team and myself. Now players have support with their strength and conditioning, which is important as the game and programme demands have increased. As a player, you have to understand what your body needs, which calls for a two-way relationship with support services. The coach needs to guide you and facilitate your learning and understanding around your needs. So the support services personnel need to understand the coach's style and approach, too. It's become far more complicated, and the art of coaching is to keep it as uncomplicated and uncluttered as possible.

There have been many changes in the wider sporting environment. The government now puts a lot of money into sport, and it wants a return on its investment. That places additional expectations around results. The coach and all the support services, particularly the sport psychologist, have to filter all that so the players don't get overwhelmed by this huge sense of responsibility.

For all that, netball has endeavoured to be a sport that's reasonably low-cost, remaining accessible to most income levels. Australia, New Zealand and England have well-funded, high-performance international netball programmes in comparison to other netball-playing nations. Jamaica and South Africa, and the countries ranked underneath Jamaica, are hugely different in terms of funding, which affects their ability to have high-performing teams year in, year out. Generally, the sport is now seen as semi-professional.

There are sociocultural factors, too. Here, women continue to play after having children, and are able to combine motherhood with high-performance sport; many of the Silver Ferns have managed this well. Netball in New Zealand has had some strong role models and leaders: women who drove the sport into the public arena, which contributed to getting live televised games as far back as the early 1970s. For women, this reframed netball as a sport for serious athletes, and not just a pastime for schoolgirls. We got into the living rooms of people throughout the country and they were starting to take notice. Thankfully, netball has preserved a positive media image (and long may that continue). Pressures of social media have created challenges for the sport to ensure that we continue to set a high standard and be respectful around how we conduct ourselves. Netball has done that really well.

There were a few male coaches when I played, but they were rare, as were male umpires. I do believe that the game can be played by men and boys, but it's currently predominantly a game played by girls and women. Outside of New Zealand, socially and in countries like Africa and the Pacific Islands, netball provides leadership opportunities, camaraderie and support for women.

In the 1979 and 1983 World Champs they did sex testing. Drug testing started in my last year as a player at the 1987 World Cup, and the procedures have advanced hugely.

In Australia, around the late 1980s or early 1990s, they had an issue where they banned a pregnant woman from playing, but they can't do that now. A woman may choose whether to play while pregnant, clearly after taking medical advice. Leanna de Bruin [née du Plooy], for example, played at up to five months pregnant in the ANZ Championships. That may have happened down the grades, but to do that at a high-performance level is rare.

Technology, too, has affected and enhanced the game. Game analysis using computer technology provides coaches and players with a lot of information. Bobby Wilcox was the first Silver Ferns video analyst to be on the bench with the coaching staff during test matches collecting live data and information. The real-time data gives coaches and players a greater understanding of the game, helping their decision-making and improving their performance. That element is going to grow. Increased use of technology in strength and conditioning, nutrition and physiotherapy, and all the support services have helped to make athletes stronger, fitter and faster.

But in the end, for me the key component is the role of the coach, and their understanding of how to mix all the ingredients together. That's the art of coaching. At one point, probably in the 1990s (and this is reflected in coach development), there was a move to focus on the sport science side of things. These elements are dynamic, but it's important that the coach's role is upheld, because in the end it's about people management and relationships. If a coach can't do that, it doesn't matter how much data they possess; they have to be able to manipulate and use that to get the performance.

Netball still has a way to go in terms of greater media coverage, especially in Australia and internationally. We have a way to go to get all international games televised or streamed live, regardless of where or when or what teams are playing. When that happens, we will know we're making some ground. I look forward to that day.

SILVER FERNS
NEW ZEALAND
vodafone

LESLEY RUMBALL

Lesley Rumball (née Nicol) played for the Silver Ferns from 1993 to 2005, representing New Zealand in 110 tests. In 1992 she was selected for the New Zealand Under 21 team, which subsequently won New Zealand's first World Youth Cup. She played in three netball World Championships (1995, 1999 and 2003), coming third, second and first, respectively. She also won silver at two Commonwealth Games (1998 and 2002), losing to Australia both times. Lesley was first made captain in 1996. She captained the Silver Ferns from 1996 to 1997 and then later in her career in 2005; she was vice-captain in 1998, 2002 and 2005. In 2004 she became an Officer of the New Zealand Order of Merit for her services to netball, and in 2016 she was inducted into the New Zealand Sport Hall of Fame at the Halberg Awards.[12]

Lesley speaks of her sense of pride in wearing the silver fern on her dress, and the powerful symbolism of the kete (where players brought personal items to share with the team when away from home). She recalls how values continued to filter through from senior leaders and pass on to the younger, newer team members. In later years leadership was shared: no single player, not even the captain, was ever relied on for this. Lesley believes the shared approach towards leadership contributed towards winning, with 'winning' as focusing on the process and team goals, rather than the score. Having spent time under several different coaches, Lesley was exposed to different coaching styles, which she believes helped her grow into a well-rounded player. There was still a battle against male sports for media coverage, but when netball games were televised free to air, this was influential for the sport, and players began to get some form of basic media training. Netball also became semi-professional at National Bank Cup level, and players were now being paid (albeit at a minimal level) to play netball.

The cultural diversity actually influences the style of play, which is different to Australia . . . and that makes the Silver Ferns different.

I was in a physiology lecture in Dunedin and I took my Walkman because the team was announced on the radio. It's funny, as they wouldn't do that these days. It must have been just after nine o'clock and, of course, the lecture started at nine. I heard the news and I was so excited. Then I sat through that whole lecture. I was in the middle of a row so I couldn't just walk out to celebrate. We finished lectures for the day and then celebrated later in the afternoon.

Looking back, it was a huge thing: I had always wanted to play for the Silver Ferns. I love netball — when I was a kid of seven or eight, I couldn't wait for the winter season to come again. I just wanted to play netball all year round. I played heaps of other sports and did quite well with them, but netball was my real passion. My mum played a lot of netball and so did my sister, so my whole life had been at netball courts. Obviously I remember watching the 1987 World Cup team and that's the one game that sticks in my mind. That was when I wanted to be a Silver Fern. So having those aspirations from quite young, it was really exciting to make the team. It had been a progressive thing, because I had made the New Zealand Under 21 team at secondary school. We played in Fiji and won the World Youth Cup. Then I made the Milo invitation team and we travelled with the Silver Ferns as training partners. So I'd slowly been getting closer and closer. It was definitely my biggest aspiration. Actually my main aspiration at that age was to go to the Olympics for the 800 and 1500 metres, but then netball took over.

Team culture

The Silver Ferns have a strong team culture which is passed on from player to player. When I first made the Silver Ferns, Leigh Gibbs was the coach and Sheryl Wells was team manager. Both Leigh and Sheryl led the induction of new players. During the induction, if it was your first time in the team and your first test match, you were presented with your playing uniform and one of the senior players gave a speech. I can picture other people over the years really vividly. I can remember Sandra Edge even though she may not have presented to me. I had looked up to her as a player for so many years and couldn't believe I was in the same team!

There had been quite a big turnover of players, and Leigh Gibbs had come in as lead coach, marking a change from Lyn Gunson. A number of us were joining the Silver Ferns from the New Zealand Under 21 team: Julie Seymour, Belinda Charteris and Linda Vagana. It was quite a special occasion, but not a big thing that was public. It was all within the team and each senior player who presented said this is what you should aspire to, this is what the silver fern means to us as a team, this is what it means to wear the uniform, to put it on and to play for New Zealand. So, the induction ceremony was quite emotional, a special moment and very much based within the team.

It stayed very similar — partly because Sheryl Wells stayed manager for most of the time. Jackie Barron was there for a short time, but mainly it was Sheryl for 12 or 13 years, so those traditions kept going through the Silver Ferns. Leigh Gibbs had played with the Silver Ferns, so she was able to carry that whole culture through, including the importance of the silver fern itself, and what it meant to wear it.

It also depended on the event, as we had a theme for each campaign. For the 2003 World Champs, each of us had a kete, a flax bag. We had all taken something special from home, and you had a buddy and you'd given something special to your buddy within the team. Throughout the tournament, that something special was symbolic of what you wanted to achieve, but you still had a little part of home: it was a reminder that we were doing this not just for us but for our country as well. So that bag was with you as a support and used in a slightly ritualistic manner.

Before going away, we'd done a lot of different scenarios of what could happen at the 2003 World Champs, and what we would do. These were called 'what ifs'. One scenario was that we'd gone to the court and the coach and manager didn't turn up, and the senior players weren't there

> I love netball — when I was a kid of seven or eight, I couldn't wait for the winter season to come again. I just wanted to play netball all year round.

either (unbeknownst to the rest of the team). The rest of the team had to take responsibility, carry on and warm up and start playing a game without anyone else there. We did this because traffic can be quite chaotic in Jamaica. We thought we would be in two buses and one of the buses might end up getting delayed going to a match.

We practised another scenario because when we were playing in the final of the Under 21 World Champs against Australia, the lights went out in the third or fourth quarter of the game and we had to sit for 20 minutes because it was too dark to play. We then had to mentally pick ourselves up and continue playing the final! So we practised all these different scenarios, a sports psychology approach, which then becomes a part of the culture so that as a player we could manage no matter what. Gilbert Enoka, a mental skills coach, was very influential throughout my playing career with the Silver Ferns and also helped formalise the team culture.

Our Otago coach, Georgie Salter, introduced lots of different themes within our teams. One year (probably everyone does it now, but not many people did it then) we did an army theme: we were sleep-deprived from working all day, but we still had to do all these mental tasks and then perform under pressure.

We also learnt the taiaha and the poi, and the associated mana and importance of them. That was about unity and applying it to teamwork. Every year with Georgie we had a new theme and that became a ritual within that team, because teams changed and evolved. Quite a few core players came through and then went on to represent New Zealand:

Anna Stanley [née Rowberry], Belinda Colling, Jo Morrison [née Steed], Victoria Edgar [née Edwards]. Belinda Charteris and Katie Fay also played for the Otago Rebels

With the Otago Rebels or Southern Steel, at the start of every season you set your team culture, you set your goals, you set your values and expectations: how you want to perform as a team, and what you expect of each player. These were written down formally. The senior player group was formed more in later years, and they either led by example or made sure that the culture was running right through the whole team. Things like always being on time, being ready for team practice, and all those expectations.

With the Silver Ferns, these things probably weren't written down initially but they definitely filtered through. As a group the senior players wrote down common goals and team expectations, which helped create the culture of the team, and that rubbed off on the younger players. The difference was that you would come together in blocks of time as opposed to doing a full season, which changes the nature of that process. Those expectations often would be related to the theme. That's why the theme comes into it so much because, rather than having the same words over and over, it brought some new edge. This would also come into the words that you used on the court, as in your keywords that you'd use. As sports psychology encourages, we had a team word that would mean you'd have to push or surge forward. It would be one single, simple word.

I was part of many teams and worked with many coaches, each with a formal process to develop team values. The process would depend on the coach, but in later years it was very much led by the senior player groups, as well as the captain and eventually by the entire team. With this wider group as part of the process, it didn't matter if a particular person wasn't on the court, because everybody stepped up and took responsibility.

I know that for the 2003 World Champs team, the key thing was that it was the same idea at the start that we had before we went into that campaign. We'd lost the 1999 World Champs, we'd lost the 2002 Commonwealth Games (though it was really close), and we knew we had to do something different. So we all sat down together (led by Ruth and Leigh) and said, we're going to take time off from whatever we're doing. I had just finished medical school, so it meant that I didn't start my first-year house surgeon position until halfway through the following year. I completed a certificate in Athlete Career Education over that six months, which was a major change compared to studying medicine.

The other issue wasn't very nice, but the team doctor basically said that as a team we were carrying too much weight. She produced a bag of potatoes and said, 'This is the extra weight you guys are carrying and you need to do something about it.' We were furious because most of us were fit! In retrospect, it was good, though, as it promoted team unity. We decided as a player group that this was inappropriate and involved our sports nutritionist to assess our skinfold/body fat over time to show changes and prove that weight itself was not relevant but lean body mass was. I was concerned as there were people in the team who were actually underweight and we didn't want this comment to promote eating disorders. So, instead of the coaches leading the next stage, the players rang Katrina Darry (a nutritionist) and said, we want you to come in because we don't agree with how this is being handled. The players took the responsibility and it was driven from within the team, whereas often the organisation is done by team management. We certainly all had buy-in.

The difference in that team was that the culture was set a year out from the World Champs, although really that team had been building for probably over six years to get to that winning point. The team changed, people came in and out, but that overall culture had remained. Ruth Aitken managed people really well, including other coaches, support people and team management — not just the players. Ruth created a team environment that was supportive but empowering. Leigh Gibbs was assistant coach. Leigh had a wealth of experience from coaching the Silver Ferns previously and is a fantastic defensive coach. We had a dedicated strength and conditioning coach, Rob Nicholson, which meant we were the fittest we had ever been. Tracey Patterson was our high-performance advisor and helped manage our lives. And Sharon Kearney, our physiotherapist, had a wealth of physiotherapy and netball knowledge, including World Champs experience, having been with the Silver Ferns for years.

The other part was the fitness. The Silver Ferns have always been fit, but this team was at another level. We agreed as a team that our fitness was going to be a differentiator, and so everyone committed to that. And that proved the difference at the 2003 World Champs.

Leadership

Leadership is crucial, but getting teams to lead themselves is even more of a skill. Not relying on just one person or on the coach: that's the key.

Lesley Rumball in action against the Australian Diamonds in the third test of the Fisher & Paykel Series in July 2004 in Hamilton. New Zealand won 53–46.
Brett O'Callaghan/ Photosport

So you can change whatever's happening on the court and adapt, whether that's led by one person, led by example, led by cue, led by something done on the court or by reading the play, and it might be more than one person who does that. It definitely contributes to a winning team, because that leadership isn't limited to the court, but extends to the culture, the expectations and all the other aspects of that team. Support is important as well, so people aren't left isolated; and then you also respect others' differences and manage those as well.

I played for Southland Country from 14 and I went to my first senior nationals at 14. The other person who had played at senior nationals at that age was Lois Muir. My Southland Country coach, Ro Brand, was brave to select a skinny, gangly 14-year-old. From there, Georgie Salter was very influential in my career. In my final year of school, I was asked by Georgie, who was the Otago coach, to go to Dunedin to play. Georgie had come down to one of our trials for Southland Country when I was in sixth form and asked if I'd like to come to Dunedin. I told my mum and dad that I didn't want to move schools, but I agreed to go in seventh form. So I was in the Otago senior team in seventh form, with Georgie as coach. When I look back at my development as a player, she was fantastic. She was inspirational and also quite out there, but it was lots of fun. She went through every skill you could have on the netball court and then you divided it up into what bit you had of that, what bit you didn't have and how you could achieve the entire skill. Other people may not respond to this approach, but I liked details; I remember having a list that ran to about eight pages, all divided up. It had everything that you would do to teach netball, and she even made you think of other things that weren't on there that you could do. Then we spent the next four or five years perfecting all of those different skills, following it right through.

Georgie taught all the different skills, tactics, and player analysis approaches. She created markedly different themes each year, and developed a very strong team culture. We not only analysed ourselves and our opposition, but also other players we wanted to aspire to. She took it to another level. These were the days when there was no one sitting on the sideline doing the analysis for you. Georgie looked at the whole player in relation to their life. Her background meant that she was holistic — growing players in every facet of the their life, not just netball. She developed our tinana (body), hinengaro (mind), whānau (team/family) and wairua (spirit). Georgie has had a huge influence on my life in so many ways and how I practice medicine is based on her approach to life. When I look back now, all those people I was with at university who were in that team, we are still really good friends. Maybe it is because you're all that same age, you're in that same environment where you're all studying.

Leigh Gibbs was my first national coach. She's really hard-working and quite tactical. I really liked her coaching. Leigh coached the Silver Ferns at the first World Champs I went to [1995]. We trained a lot, including the morning before a game. This probably wouldn't happen now with the increasing sports science knowledge about training load, but traditionally players trained hard the day of games. In retrospect, as players it was also a lesson to speak up. Leigh came back as assistant coach under Ruth and we won World Champs in 2003. Leigh is very meticulous: we had individual player plans and she went through everything that makes you as a player and worked through them, making improvements.

Yvonne Willering was very strong on team culture: you're doing it for your country and for the Silver Ferns. She used drills more than my previous coaches, and taught a different type of defence, which was good. Leigh's approach was initially tight woman-on-woman and her style evolved over the years; then there was Georgie, who did woman-to-woman, woman-to-space, presence, directing and space/zone. This was very technical, which I loved. Georgie was great at putting scenarios into court/playing situations. However, Yvonne was very zone-focused and she really helped me develop this aspect of my game. As a player, having these different styles made it easy to adapt to different teams and situations. During a game we would adapt our play without external input from the coach. As players we would discuss what style to use against various teams, rather than just having a coach tell you what to do. Georgie intentionally developed this ability in her players. Ruth, Leigh and Robyn [Broughton] all empowered players to make these tactical changes. A coach might not tell us; we just did it. That's probably why we did well with all three defensive approaches. All those things you learn over the years: you put it together, and you develop into a winning team.

For the New Zealand Under 21s we had Leigh and Georgie and I thought they worked well together as a combination. Ruth's more of an attacking coach; she also brought everyone together, and made the most of everyone around her. She managed people really well and created a winning environment through meticulous planning and selecting the right people at the right time in terms of the support people. It's like being a football manager in some ways, but it's crucial to creating that winning environment.

I do think coaching style depends on the age and experience of their players. When you're older, you realise that you can actually manage a lot yourself, but just need someone who keeps the team together and manages people within the team. Robyn Broughton is a coach [Southern Sting, 1998–2007] who excels at managing people, especially players who may have not done well with other teams. She'd bring players into her team and they'd excel. That's managing personalities within the team, and knowing what makes them tick. She is good at using the knowledge of other players and senior leadership. She probably did that a little bit before her time, and when you look back at the Southern Sting, they won seven years in a row. I'm sure her coaching style was a big part of it. She's just so good at getting the best out of her players, as well as being strong in terms of the technical and tactical components. So that's not just the coaching on the court, it's also off-court management. When players feel that they want to do it not only for themselves but also for the team and coach, that makes a big difference. There are so many factors, though. You might have a fantastic coach, but not have the players at that point, or they might lack experience. The stars need to align. There's always other factors involved, or there might be one crucial injury in the year that changes the dynamics.

I was really young when I was first made captain of the Silver Ferns. Looking back, I can't believe I was picked so young. I was 22 and had experience as Otago captain. It probably was a bit soon for me at that level, but the opportunity came up because there were retirements. It was quite hard because we lost the senior players. So I got into the team in 1994 and within two years I became captain. Lots of people in the team were older or more experienced than me. It was a brave move by Leigh Gibbs. In part I presume I was chosen for my commitment: I trained hard and worked hard. I was always looking for something else to improve on, and would lead by example. I don't know if I was quite ready to deal with the media at 22 years old. I guess that you learn on the job, and I was probably quite naïve when I look back. However, you learn from your mistakes and I was very resilient. I grew into the captaincy role with experience gained from being Otago Rebels captain and Southern Sting captain through successive National Bank Cup wins.

Then Yvonne came in as coach and dropped me as captain. I wasn't really meant to make the team at all when the Silver Ferns went to England [in 1997] and I was on the sidelines for the first part of the first game. We were losing so she brought me on and, not that I made the difference, but the team turned itself around. I had to fight just for my place back in the team with Yvonne, though I did end up being vice-captain a couple of years later. That was interesting: Bernie [Bernice Mene] was captain, I was vice-captain and Belinda [Colling] had been a captain. So we had had quite a few captains over time. When we went to the World Champs in 2003, there was a leadership group that had all been captain at some stage.

I was asked to be captain again when Adine Wilson [née Harper] got injured. This was much later in my career [2005] and I said no, I don't want to be captain; if you really wanted me to be captain you'd have named me before now, so I'm just a fill-in. I'm happy to do my leadership bit but not carry that label. Somehow they convinced me to. In some ways it took the load off the younger ones, I guess. In the end I agreed because I don't think it changed what I did in the team at all, other than being seen in the public eye. Otherwise you're doing pretty much the same role because you had so much input tactically and also at training as a senior player. That load was spread; it was never just one person driving it all because I don't think that's a healthy team culture.

WD

Our team communication evolved over time as I became more experienced as a captain. We'd have team meetings, captain meetings, player meetings, senior player groups with Ruth and Leigh, management meetings. There was lots of face-to-face communication. That all takes up quite a lot of time, but it's important. You need to make it fun and interesting so it's not just the same routine; you're kind of rehashing but doing it in different ways. That was really well done at the World Champs in 2003. Before we went away, we got into different groups, and the manager would write a to-do list, and each member would be responsible for particular tasks. It might be allocating the laundry, for instance, or managing and checking the food. Then the manager would feed back to the rest of the team: are you happy with this? So everyone felt like they had buy-in, rather than just someone at the top saying this is what you will do. There was also the entertainment group. We did different team activities, say every two days, and that group was responsible for managing that and running ideas past the whole team. So it wasn't led just by the management; everything within the team was team-driven. There was much more responsibility, and, of course, it became slightly competitive as well.

Emphasis on winning

One of the most influential wins of my career was at the World Youth Champs in 1991. We hadn't previously won at Under 21 level and everyone thought Australia would win, because they normally beat Under 21 teams by a big score. Another was winning at the World Champs in 2003, because we worked so hard to get there and we had been so close for so long.

On the other side, there was losing in the Commonwealth Games in Kuala Lumpur in 1998, and again in Manchester in 2002. At Manchester, the final went into extra time so we had another quarter, and then we lost in extra time after the fifth quarter. That was where we said, hang on a minute: that loss is what we needed. And that was such an influence on the World Champs in 2003. Even though Bubby [Temepara George] got sent off part-way through the game, so we didn't have a centre, not once did I think we were going to lose it. I felt like that the whole way through; the thing is having complete faith in your team — no matter what, we were going to do it.

With the Southern Steel we had that same feeling, and that obviously builds up over time. A lot of factors come into it. It doesn't matter what happens to you; the could-haves and would-haves don't matter. Whatever happened, we just managed it. We had complete faith in the other players. Normally when something goes wrong, people get their heads down, but no one ever did that. You get that perfect performance; it's like you're almost not there, you're almost outside watching yourself do it. You might only get that once in your career. For me, it was based on having very high standards. We all wanted to be the best in the world, and I felt that even if we had a team that wasn't experienced, we'd never settle for second best.

But focusing on winning is a dangerous thing to fall into. It affects how you train, and that affects how you play, and it affects your expectations. It isn't just the winning; it's about how you win, what you do as you go through everything, your process goals, and then what you do on the court. What you do in the lead-up prior to going onto the court determines whether you win — leaving no stone unturned.

Against Australia, we do pretty well. If they lose a couple of players they've got exactly the same standard of players waiting to come in, whereas we have the top ones playing and have a bigger drop-off to that next group down. Those players have to work quite hard to get up to the standard needed at international level, and so the turnover of top players is quite significant for us. It doesn't impact on Australia so much because of the size of their player pool. Also, the people who do get into the Australian team are ruthless, because they wouldn't have got there otherwise. Sometimes you might get put out against these players before you're ready. But if we get to keep a core of people who go right through, which we've done each time when we've won, then we are successful. If you look at New Zealand overall, we probably do punch above our weight. By population, in lots of different sports, especially recent Olympic results, we have high expectations and so does the public. That means that as athletes you are expected to do well, which is good because it makes you work that much harder.

Environmental factors

The media are an important part of the game. There was never a time that management said we were unavailable for interviews; we were always available. Management were very good at accommodating any requests, which is quite different to, say, the All Blacks, who are very structured. Partly this was because we knew as females that we needed the media exposure, and we needed our sport to have that, too. Another part was that you were always available after games for signing autographs.

Coverage for women's sport was better in the late 1990s than today, I think. Back then, you could open the newspaper and you'd see a number of stories on women's sport, but if you look now — it's really poor. That's looking at all women's sport, not just netball. They should have a similar number of stories to men's sport. Because of this, we were very accessible to the media. Requests would go through the manager, but it's very seldom that we would turn anything down.

The fact that games were free to air was very influential for netball. Even the National Bank Cup was on at seven at night, on prime-time television, and the final would be on TV for everyone to see, and it would be in pubs. That's really influential on young people who want to play netball. And it was live, rather than just delayed coverage.

With any sport, the media is important if you want to grow your sport, and it's important with sponsorship. The demands of media have probably increased over the years, but I don't think they were too onerous when I was playing. You might do a post-match interview or some interviews beforehand, but you got to know everyone really well and it's quite fun. Often there were things that you knew were going to be controversial, but there wasn't just one person coming out with it: you were all coming from the same background on a topic. I guess it's why there wasn't too much controversy. We did do media training when we were younger: about how to be yourself and be natural. I remember Glenda Hughes coming into one camp to practise a scenario where someone had been caught sunbathing topless and how would you respond to it. That media training probably came in in the early to mid-1990s.

With the Silver Ferns, compared to [a number of] other women's sports at that time, all of our flights were paid for, our trips were paid for, and you didn't have to fund it yourself. Also, a Prime Minister's Scholarship [awarded to promising athletes to help support themselves through study] meant that I could stop work. I didn't work as a house surgeon for the first part of the year before the World Champs in 2003. I had studied medicine and played, so that meant that when I took that time off I could apply for a Prime Minister's Scholarship. I did a diploma in athlete career education through the University of Victoria in Melbourne part-time, but it meant that I didn't have to work the hours of a house surgeon, which was 50-hour weeks, and train. The Prime Minister's Scholarships came in when I was studying medicine, part-way through my netball career.

I was really lucky to be in that era. We began to get paid at franchise level and at New Zealand level near the end of my playing career. We called it 'semi-professional' at National Bank Cup level (now the ANZ Championship). So you were starting to get paid, but you could still develop a career outside of netball, and come out with something at the end. As an athlete, if you have nothing other than your sport and you get an injury, or something goes wrong or you don't get selected, it's hard to manage if you don't have something else to focus on. It's tough if you just have your identity as a netballer. When you retire from the game you need a plan in place. That is harder to do now because you can probably only study part-time due to the level of commitment needed to train and play. So even though at the time it was really, really hard financially, potentially

I had the best of both worlds. Payment [playing at the cup level] probably isn't a lot more and I was able to complete a physiotherapy degree, then a medical degree while still playing netball. Our hours of training were similar to what players do now but perhaps our training wasn't as effective, as we didn't have the recovery time to get the benefit from hard training. In my day you could develop a career and probably be a better person for it because you were not focused solely on netball.

When I was with Otago we'd fundraise. In the Otago Rebels, Jo Steed [now Morrison] made our uniforms. She sewed all of our dresses! This was the start of netballers wearing dresses again. Everyone pitched in and contributed to the team. We fundraised to go away to nationals, which you don't do these days. Those things developed a culture within the team, because you had to do extra things and become self-reliant.

Fisher & Paykel came in as a major sponsor of netball, and that followed through for quite a few years. Sponsorship is crucial. Netball New Zealand had funding through what would have been SPARC, and is now High Performance Sport New Zealand. Funding was dependent on how well you did at World Champs. There's probably more potential for individual sponsorship now, whereas everything was quite team-based then. This is again important in creating a team culture; everyone's on a level footing. That is, on court everyone is as good as each other, but if one person is getting big sponsorship then this might change the dynamic and make them think they are better than the others in the team.

That's why team sponsorship is crucial and why we did a lot with our sponsors. It was important to be available. It was outside of training and playing commitments, but you went along happily because you knew that was crucial for the funding. Duckie [Sheryl Wells] was a very good team manager. If you went to a function, and the sponsors were there, or maybe at the after-match function, she was very good at checking that you were all in twos, and you'd have to tell her how many of the sponsors you'd talked to, rather than people just congregating in the corner. Everyone had to move around and 'work the room'.

WD

Culture, too, is an important part of being a Silver Fern. We always sung a waiata as a team because that was important to us as players. Everywhere we went, we sang; you then realised that you knew all these songs.

At the World Champs, they have a candle lighting ceremony at the start where lots of countries go up and do their national dance — and so that was, of course, one of the forums for our waiata. But generally after the game, when you're away at nationals, you would also do a waiata or a performance. With the strong Samoan and Fijian presence, and a mixed Polynesian influence as well, that builds the character within the team.

There is also quite a religious side that comes in, and you do things that are important to each player. That was where the kete idea was quite good because you presented your kete and you said, this is what is important to me, this is what it means to me to be a Silver Fern, this is why I have these things in my kete. You may have known a player for a really long time, and you take things for granted, and this was a nice way to find out something new. The cultural diversity also influences the style of play, which is different to Australia, who in the past were not such a culturally diverse team.

We do well when we play a really powerful, dynamic game. You might call it flair. That's what the New Zealand style is and when we are fit enough to play it, that's when we beat Australia. We don't just compete in the same way, we don't do the same things as them: we play a different style and that's our strength. We change the timing, as they play on a very similar timing — like land, one, two, pass — and that is part of that cultural diversity that makes the Silver Ferns different. It does influence the team culture and vision.

All of the relationships established in netball, and its culture and values, have shaped my life. Those experiences play such a role in what you end up doing, where you go, and those friendships stay forever.

WD

Pregnancy was an interesting episode — it is an inherent part of female sports. I was 16 weeks pregnant when I played my last National Bank Cup final. I had returned to fitness quickly, but didn't get my contract renewed the following season because I'd had a C-section. On that occasion the decision was made by a female administrator, which I disagreed with. These days it would be the role of a doctor to make decisions on fitness for contracts.

The whole family/whānau culture is really important in New Zealand netball, again partly because we're a smaller country. When you're a kid you go to the netball courts with your family, and that all flows through. My mum, Alwyn, played a huge role in my netball career — she also played representative netball and coached Southland Country. My mum, Mumma (my grandmother) and my dad travelled all over the world to support my netball.

BERNICE MENE

Bernice Mene represented New Zealand between 1992 and 2001, playing 78 tests. She was first drafted into the Silver Ferns squad in 1991 as a 17-year-old schoolgirl. In 1992 she toured England with the Silver Ferns and played in every test. In 1997, aged 22, she became the Silver Ferns' nineteenth captain. After injury, Bernice returned to the team in 1999 and resumed the captaincy role during 2000–01. She represented the Silver Ferns at two Netball World Cups (1995 and 1999) and the 1998 Commonwealth Games. She was appointed a member of the New Zealand Order of Merit for services to netball in 2003.[13]

In her interview, Bernice noted the importance of the culture in team sports, and how that culture changed during her 10 years in the Silver Ferns. At times it was affected by different personalities, but it thrived on a good mix of young and experienced players. During her time as a player, mental skills training was introduced, and values were discussed as a team but were still not formally written down. Leadership groups, likewise, were utilised but were not formal; they consisted of a core group of senior players who were perceived to help contribute significantly towards a winning team. Winning was judged by the outcome of the game, and, as ever, the Ferns' success was measured mainly by comparison to Australia. The cultural make-up of the team was also considered very special due to the ethnic diversity of players, and the flair of these players was upheld as a key team strength.

You're judged on the outcome, so winning is super important . . . your results against Australia are your biggest measurements.

It wasn't a conventional way of finding out I was in the Silver Ferns. A local reporter rang and said, 'Congratulations.' I knew nothing of what she was talking about. She ended up saying, 'Oh, um, sorry, it's embargoed until six o'clock tonight,' or it may have been the next day. So she told me and then I told Dad. Mum was out at parent/teacher/student interviews because she was a teacher at my school. All of the media stuff happened the next day. It was funny, because these days your first notification would be from Netball New Zealand. I had no idea of how it was going to impact on me. For those around me, it meant more to them. Dad started crying, and from his reaction I thought that this must be a really big thing, because he never cried.

I had always wanted to represent New Zealand. I imagined that it would be in athletics, so it felt like a natural progression when I started playing netball. Even when I first started, people asked, 'Is this the next Silver Fern?' I'm not sure which magazine it was, but we were only 11 and they selected all these athletes from different sports — there may have been 12 of us — and quite a few did come through and compete for New Zealand in their chosen sport. I'd only just started playing netball, so I thought that was really weird.

Team culture

Team culture is obviously big in a team sport and it really changed in the 10 years that I was in the team. When I first came into the side, there were some strong personalities and some power clashes over where people thought they would be or should have been on the court. That can be destructive. We were losing by big, big margins and you can't afford to be thinking in that way; you need to be working towards the same goal, as opposed to thinking of yourself or getting on the court.

I don't think there was a team belief at that stage that we could win. Players verbalised it, but I don't know if they meant it or believed it. Later, there was more of a nurturing of the young players coming through and an appreciation of people's differences and what they brought to the team. The coach and management didn't sell that true belief that the players in the team had done the work and that we could, as a team, beat the opposition.

A good team is a mix of experience and youth, because the young players bring a passion and excitement for the game and that rubs off on the older players, but then you also need the maturity and knowledge of the older players to guide them through. Every coach has a different team. They need to build their own team; that's important. Every coach also has their own captain who they choose to work with, and this is a pivotal relationship.

GK

My first experience with the Silver Ferns was on a tour to Australia. I met everyone for the first time at a marae, which was the only formal ceremonial sort of induction. After a few years, when I had been in the team for a while, they started to give out test uniforms — the test dresses. There would be an official handing-over of the test uniform to the players, and this made it more ceremonial. But when I first got into the team there wasn't as much of this. It was more talking about the need to be tough in the Silver Ferns to make the court. That you had to work really hard, and if you weren't playing (in the test match), then the next day, you would do training so you knew how hard it was for the players who had played the night before. It was an interesting culture when I first came in. It was very hierarchical and we were losing to Australia quite a lot, so they were trying to really impress upon us the work ethic and how much you needed to work to beat Australia.

At test-match time there would be new player press releases, which we started when I was captaining. We went to press functions and, for example, when Irene [van Dyk] and Vilimaina [Davu] arrived, we were all together with the coaching staff to announce that. We did do more of an induction through [Silver Ferns manager] Sheryl Wells, like learning the national anthem, how to mix and mingle, post-match functions, how to be professional in appearance, representing New Zealand, and those sorts of things. It was a more formal approach, as opposed to people assuming that you knew what you were meant to do.

Obviously, the silver fern was our big symbol. At home, I still have a little silver fern badge that I got from the Under 21s, and one from the Silver Ferns, so a lot of onus is put on that legacy. Only those who had played for New Zealand got those. It was only when netball came into the Commonwealth Games that it dawned on us that we were part of a bigger scheme: a New Zealand team within a greater New Zealand team. It is a real honour to be one of 12 who are representing all netball in New Zealand. The dress with the silver fern was your big thing, and post-career it was a big thing to have it signed by your teammates.

Everyone had their own pre-match rituals and routines, but all teams were regimented in terms of training, playing, food, training logs, measurements and fitness. A lot of the procedure on test-match day was like clockwork as well. We would always have a walk-through in the morning, and enforced rests; food was really important, including the pre-match meal. Some people liked to prepare in different ways, mentally as well.

During my time, when Leigh Gibbs came in as coach [1994], we did a lot of blackboard mental skills sessions with mental skills coach Gilbert Enoka, and we did quite a bit with him on values. They were verbalised, but I don't know if they were written down. When I was with PIC [Pacific Island Church] in Wellington, we carried with us a book that had our values and rules in the front of our training bags all season. If we veered from them, it was pulled up and pointed out in those books. Definitely, it was something we went over together. With Southland, it was always pre-season; that was the first thing we addressed, to make sure everyone was on the same page.

Leadership

There's no way you're going to be a winning team without a good, strong leadership group, and that comes from the coach, the captain and the senior players. Everyone's contribution is important; as is knowing their role and playing their part.

When I became captain [in 1997] we had had a change of coach. Wai Taumaunu and Yvonne Willering had come in as coaching staff. They asked me to come back as captain, after I had had an injury. In terms of leadership style, I had been captain, and vice-captain, quite early on for Canterbury and then I had captained the Under 21 national team as well. It was consistency; I was earning my position on court and getting that bib. I had had quite a few knee injuries, and so when I came back to captain the team my knee wasn't 100 per cent, but I pushed on. I had an operation and was back playing Australia in under four weeks. Consequently, my body was falling apart and I was struggling with training, so I ended up not going on the summer tour to the UK because I thought it was important to start from scratch and get my body back. If you're not performing, then you don't really have the confidence to lead as a captain. So I relinquished the captaincy. Belinda Colling took that on and she was great. She was Yvonne's captain from then through to the World Champs, after which they asked me to come back in as captain.

We didn't have a special leadership group per se. We had a core of senior players, like Lesley Nicol [now Rumball], who was captain before me and remained in the team throughout. When I was there, Belinda Colling was still playing, so we had consistent performers who had good leadership skills in each area of the court. Although we didn't call them the leadership group, they were my sounding boards and support crew, and they all led when required. I had Linda Vagana behind me as well — we had a really good core group.

With communication being a massive thing in any team, the coach and captain would meet and review at the end of each day. But it was the captain's job to keep an eye on how the team was progressing by looking at the individuals, and looking after motivation and media. The vice-captain role was very much a support role, sharing that load.

GK

I played under Lyn Gunson to start with, then Leigh Gibbs and then Yvonne Willering. Yvonne also had a few different assistant coaches. There was Wai Taumaunu and Robyn Broughton. I played under all of them in a regional team, and then when Ruth [Aitken] came in I retired. I didn't

Bernice Mene at the 1999 World Championships in Christchurch. New Zealand lost the final against Australia by one point. *Photosport*

have the energy to begin again, because every time you get a new coach, it's a real new culture restart, and a rebuild. I was literally on my last legs when Ruth came in. Everyone else said it was a shock when I retired at that stage, but I thought I had done pretty well to hang in there for 10 years, because after my first year I had my major knee injury and the medical profession had told me to not play anymore. I had to retrain to walk and run from scratch. So to see out 10 years was pretty good.

I had been under Leigh for Canterbury from the beginning. Leigh was known for driving a really high work ethic, and we were always the fittest side. She took that into the Silver Ferns as well, so I always had that base and we always had a very high standard. She worked hard with us as a team. She raised the training and work ethic, breaking down the skills.

All of these coaches had played for New Zealand themselves, and their playing style was reflected in their coaching style, which was each of their strengths. Lyn was very practical, and about mentally beating the opposition: figuring things out, analysing the competition, their strengths and weaknesses, and then breaking down your role on the court. Yvonne was a flamboyant player, not that I watched her play, but she was in defence. Actually, all of them were in defence: Leigh was more of a midcourt defence, Lyn was that midcourt defence as well, and Yvonne was a goal defence/goal keep, which was my position. She promoted going for intercepts. She wanted the team to be fit prior to coming into the Silver Ferns, like her. Her mantra was that it wasn't her job to get the team fit; the onus was on us. I could understand that theory, and she had a lot of success with it. Wai was a goal defence as well, and I loved her approach.

In the Silver Ferns and in high-performance coaching, a lot of coaches have come out of the defensive end and from a defensive background, which is interesting. There are only a few shooting coaches. It's important to surround yourself with a good coaching support team, in the form of assistant coaches and specialist coaches.

Emphasis on winning

You're judged on the outcome, so winning is super important. We get all of the pressure on us to win from the public, but it's also important in terms of funding. No one really cares if the team is improving. Your results against Australia are your biggest measurement. We had a win in South Africa where we beat Australia and South Africa [2000]; it was a really good

Tri-Series. The fact that we were away as well was great; it was a cool team.

At the big tournaments the goals eluded us, but in some ways your mark moves slightly as you get older, as a senior player in the team. I did achieve some amazing things in my time. Sometimes when you won against Australia it was more relief that you felt as opposed to elation. We always believed that we could win and that we had the ability to do so, but it was really about proving it to everyone else. We knew we could do it, but not for that 'we were the best in the world' feeling. It's not really like that when you get there. I imagine it's like climbing Everest.

At the 1999 World Champs in Christchurch we were definitely a much better team than Australia. We were up with a couple of minutes to go, and then they turned it around. The crowd was massive, we were on home turf, and we had had a really good build-up. We'd done everything possible, and then for us to lose in the final few seconds . . . It replayed over and over in everyone's heads, after four years working towards that moment. The whole crowd were on their feet in silence at the end of the match. You always think about it. You try to blank it out, but it's still there.

Size and depth-wise Australia are bigger, and they had the infrastructure before us. They had their academy [the Australian Institute of Sport] and they have a stronger competition because of their numbers, the regions and the state sides. People talk about the Aussies being tougher, mentally tougher. We used to try to replicate that. The styles have diluted quite a lot over time. International netball has become more international and more accessible, and even the English style has changed [with more of them playing in the Australian competition].

Environmental factors

The national competition changed quite a lot. I was lucky to play under some great coaches and players, legends like Sandra Edge and Noeline Taurua. My time spanned a lot of players, such as Adine Wilson [née Harper] and there was Donna Loffhagen [now Wilkins] and Belinda Colling, both with their basketball [national team] and their netball.

There were changes in how the game was played with regards to speed and style. When Irene came in she struggled with the speed at which our midcourters passed, and there were adjustments for both our players and Irene. There's a lot more height at either end of the court now. We've had stages where there were just big bombs [i.e., long, high passes] into the goal shoot, so the defence had to adjust to that. On a world scale, Australia and New Zealand coaches have gone out into the South Pacific and over to the UK. Some Caribbean basketball players have come in and played in our competition, so it has globalised in many ways, but still only in Commonwealth countries. In saying that, the coaching that has gone overseas has affected netball in areas in Asia and the Pacific.

South Africa came back in, as they weren't part of world netball then. I remember the first match, as they had not been included in world netball for years. For their players, it was pretty monumental. For us to go and tour South Africa was big. Even now, I think they have a lack of continuity for their players coming through. South African players, like Leana [de Bruin] and Irene, came across because they were building new lives and it was an opportunity for them to come to New Zealand.

Fiji had their coups and so forth, and so Vilimaina [Davu] came for the opportunity as well. We've always had a really good mix of Pacific Island players and that's added to New Zealand's strength and flair, and given us a different style compared to, say, the Australian team, or even England. We were always good with culture. Tikanga Māori and language were impressed upon us, as well as knowing the national anthem and protocols. We made a lot of marae visits and there was a proper acceptance of culture.

GK

The ability to video and review games, and for the players to be able to create their own profiles on social media, that's been a change. There is a lot of analysis, shot analysis and apps that can support the players now, and sophisticated GPS tracking of players on court. When it went to Sky and the ANZ Champs, there was more netball on TV, and being able to replay things over and over is important. We always had analysis, but it was VCR.

As for media, we were taught how to deal with them — 'be good to them and they'll be good to us'. A lot of ex-players have gone through to commentary and fronting, which has been a good pathway. And netball, compared to other sports, has had some very consistent sponsors, too. In my time, Fisher & Paykel and Vodafone were big. The media sponsors always play a massive part in the sport, and other countries were quite envious of the support we had. There were always car sponsors, and on an individual basis a few of our players have been getting quite good endorsements.

Silver Fern captain Casey Kopua talking to a reporter, 2015. Learning how to work with the media has become an increasingly important leadership skill for captains and senior players in the last two decades. *Michael Bradley*

PART 4

Growth and athlete-centred semi-professionalism 2002–2019

The trend towards professionalism in netball, which began in the previous era, has continued since 2002. The initiation of the ANZ Championship in 2008 made the dream of being a full-time netballer, at least for part of the year, a reality for those players contracted to New Zealand franchises. The number of international matches also increased significantly. To some degree, players were compensated by receiving payments towards their living costs, but even for most 'professional' players the incomes received were modest, especially compared to men's sports. Moreover, government funding for high-performance sport came with corresponding expectations that this would be matched by on-court success. Coaches and captains also needed to juggle their obligations towards sponsors and the media, which increased significantly.

It is a tribute to the skill of those entrusted with leadership positions in the Silver Ferns that netball retained its position as the most popular team sport for women. It remains the only women's team sport that receives significant media coverage. The advent of social media allowed players to increase their profile, and for some this could be another income stream. With greater accessibility, however, came greater scrutiny, particularly when the team was not performing well. The principles of inclusiveness and pride in selection have been reaffirmed in this era, with a more accommodating approach to pregnant players and those with young families.

The twenty-first century started promisingly for the Silver Ferns, particularly between 2003 and 2010, when they won the World Championships in 2003 and the Commonwealth Games gold medal in 2006 and 2010. Since then, success has been harder to come by. Australia remain the dominant force in international netball, but the game is also becoming more competitive globally. England, who won the gold medal at the 2018 Commonwealth Games; Caribbean nations, such as Jamaica; and African teams, such as South Africa and Malawi (who defeated New Zealand at the 2018 Commonwealth Games), have all improved significantly and pose a major challenge to the Silver Ferns.

TABLE 5: NEW ZEALAND VS AUSTRALIA, 2002–15

YEAR	EVENT	NZ SCORE	AUS SCORE	WINNER
2002	XVII Commonwealth Games	55	57	AUS
2003	11th World Championships	49	47	NZL
2004	Fisher & Paykel Series	54	45	NZL
2004	Fisher & Paykel Series	52	50	NZL
2004	Fisher & Paykel Series	53	46	NZL
2004	Holden Astra Test Series	49	54	AUS
2004	Holden Astra Test Series	50	42	NZL
2004	Holden Astra Test Series	51	53	AUS
2005	Holden Astra Test	50	43	NZL
2005	Fisher & Paykel Test	61	36	NZL
2006	XVIII Commonwealth Games	60	55	NZL
2006	Holden Test Series	52	40	NZL
2006	Holden Test Series	38	48	AUS
2006	Fisher & Paykel Series	47	51	AUS
2006	Fisher & Paykel Series	43	37	NZL
2006	Fisher & Paykel Series	40	46	AUS
2007	Tri-Nations Series	47	50	AUS
2007	Fisher & Paykel Series	46	53	AUS
2007	Holden Test Series	67	65	NZ
2007	Holden Test Series	47	54	AUS
2007	12th World Championships	38	42	AUS
2008	New World Series	51	53	AUS
2008	New World Series	38	31	NZL
2008	Holden Test Series	46	41	NZL
2008	Holden Test Series	41	43	AUS
2009	Holden Test Series	53	50	NZL
2009	Holden Test Series	44	48	AUS
2009	Holden Test Series	33	36	AUS
2009	New World Series	46	47	AUS
2009	New World Series	52	36	NZL

continued page 146

2010	Holden Netball Test Series	43	48	AUS
2010	Constellation Cup New World Series	59	40	NZL
2010	Constellation Cup New World Series	40	46	AUS
2010	XIX Commonwealth Games	66	64	NZL
2011	Constellation Cup New World Series	47	52	AUS
2011	Constellation Cup New World Series	45	42	NZL
2011	13th World Championships	57	58	AUS
2011	Holden Netball Test Series	49	48	NZL
2011	Holden Netball Test Series	44	51	AUS
2011	Holden Netball Test Series	41	44	AUS
2012	Constellation Cup New World Series	54	52	NZL
2012	Constellation Cup New World Series	50	49	NZL
2012	Constellation Cup New World Series	53	59	AUS
2012	Holden Netball Quad Series	48	68	AUS
2012	Holden Netball Quad Series	48	43	NZL
2013	Constellation Cup New World Series	55	51	NZL
2013	Constellation Cup New World Series	45	48	AUS
2013	Coles Constellation Cup Series	50	50	DRAW
2013	Coles Constellation Cup Series	47	52	AUS
2013	Coles Constellation Cup Series	49	50	AUS
2014	XX Commonwealth Games	40	58	AUS
2014	Constellation Cup New World Series	42	59	AUS
2014	Real Insurance Constellation Cup Series	40	49	AUS
2014	Real Insurance Constellation Cup Series	34	47	AUS
2014	Constellation Cup New World Series	47	51	AUS
2015	14th World Championships Pool	52	47	NZL
2015	14th World Championships	55	58	AUS
2015	Constellation Cup New World Series	44	50	AUS
2015	Constellation Cup New World Series	48	58	AUS
2015	Constellation Cup New World Series	50	47	NZL
2015	Constellation Cup New World Series	58	47	NZL

TABLE 6: NEW ZEALAND VS AUSTRALIA, 2016–19

YEAR	EVENT	NZ SCORE	AUS SCORE	WIN
2016	Netball Quad Series	55	60	AUS
2016	Constellation Cup	56	68	AUS
2016	Constellation Cup	53	51	NZL
2016	Constellation Cup	50	62	AUS
2016	Constellation Cup	45	49	AUS
2017	Netball Quad Series	50	57	AUS
2017	Netball Quad Series	57	47	NZL
2017	Constellation Cup	54	57	AUS
2017	Constellation Cup	52	60	AUS
2017	Constellation Cup	43	55	AUS
2017	Constellation Cup	42	58	AUS
2018	Netball Quad Series	48	67	AUS
2018	XXI Commonwealth Games	44	65	AUS
2018	Netball Quad Series	55	60	AUS
2018	Constellation Cup	42	57	AUS
2018	Constellation Cup	47	56	AUS
2018	Constellation Cup	55	44	NZL
2018	Constellation Cup	47	58	AUS
2019	Netball Quad Series	50	53	AUS
2019	World Cup	49	50	AUS
2019	World Cup	52	51	NZL
2019	Constellation Cup	53	52	NZL
2019	Constellation Cup	42	48	AUS
2019	Constellation Cup	54	53	NZL
2019	Constellation Cup	46	53	AUS

Source: https://www.silverferns.co.nz/silver-ferns/history/results.html

SILVER FERNS
NEW ZEALAND

RUTH AITKEN

Ruth Aitken (née Fathers) represented New Zealand at the 1979 World Netball Championships in Trinidad and Tobago. In 2002 she began coaching the Silver Ferns, the eighth to coach the team. During Aitken's tenure as national head coach, the Silver Ferns won the 2003 World Netball Championships and the 2006 and 2010 Commonwealth Games, but came second to Australia at both the 2002 Commonwealth Games and the 2007 and 2011 World Netball Championships. She is the most capped Silver Ferns coach, with 112 tests, winning 87 for a 77 per cent success rate over 10 years.[14]

In 2011 Aitken was named an Officer of the New Zealand Order of Merit.[15] She has remained involved in the game. In December 2012 Aitken was appointed to a new role as Technical Director and National Coach of Netball Singapore. Under her coaching, Singapore won the 2014 Asian Netball Championships and the netball competition at the 2015 Southeast Asian Games.[16] In 2016 the Netball Waikato Bay of Plenty Zone appointed Aitken as a performance manager, with the focus of the programme being to educate coaches and players by providing a pathway to high-performance netball.

In her interview Ruth describes how a more formal induction process was introduced, with the presentation of the Silver Fern dress becoming a significant ritual. Team culture continued to be handed down consistently, thanks to there being a stable group of players, and values were passed down by imitation: these were identified as respecting the fern, contributing to the team, demonstrating resilience, and being a Silver Fern 24/7. A shared leadership approach was favoured, with a strong belief that everyone needed to contribute to the team in order for it to do well and win. In coaching, the empowerment approach was considered an effective way to tap into what each player brought to the team. Also, the trend towards a more semi-professional environment was seen to have helped players significantly; being paid to play enabled them to lead more normal lives and train at normal hours.

Shared leadership is more important than one good leader . . . It's about growing leadership within the group.

I was selected as a national player for only one tournament, the 1979 World Netball Championships in Trinidad. In those days, they didn't run a national squad at all. They picked a team for the Worlds, and the following year there was no team picked because there were no international matches scheduled. Then, the following year, Te Aroha Keenan kicked me out as we were both shooters! I got dropped and she was selected. Later, she got dropped and Adrianne Hayes was selected as a shooter. All three of us ended up being national selectors together, so we were looking at each other saying, 'You were the one that put me out of the Silver Ferns!' We thought it was really funny.

It was the good old days, when you travelled to Wellington for two days of trials on outdoor courts, and then they brought everyone into the room at the end of trials and read out a list of names of those selected. If they read out your name, you stayed in the room and were given information about the tour. If they didn't, you walked outside and went to see your family. We've come a long way since then, luckily. My maiden name was Fathers, so there were a couple of names read out before mine. Two years later, I went back to trials after I married and became Aitken. Then, in the calling out of the names, they went to a B name first up and I thought, 'I've missed out!'

Team culture

When I was coach, a senior player would be involved in the initiation or the induction of a junior player when they first arrived in camp. We would say our introductions in a circle, and then all go round and welcome the new player with a kiss and a hug. We would make sure that everyone was welcomed before they came into the group, prior to their first training. Later in the camp, we would have a small dress ceremony where the playing dress and tracksuit were presented by one of the senior players, who would then talk about the new player and what she brought to the team.

We acknowledged their first test match with a card that we all wrote in. These cards really made our new caps aware of how special it was to join the team. Senior players help those coming in to understand the importance of being a Silver Fern, how to behave, and the importance of respecting the silver fern.

A really nice thing about the Silver Ferns is that you have players who have been there for a long time. There will be some who, unfortunately, come in and leave quite quickly, and some go out and then come back in once they realise how much harder they have to work to stay in the team; but the legacy and consistency are important. It's a lot easier to hand a team culture down when you have a stable group. One advantage of being a coach over a number of years was that I could add a little more value all the time, because sometimes it's hard to start everything. It's about how it grows naturally out of the group as well. To be honest, a lot of the stuff I instigated came from the ideas of the players and then I picked them up and ran with them. It certainly wasn't all because of me.

A symbol that I really related to for that 2003 campaign was 'the rock', which was seen as being strong and stable. We had a few sessions with Gilbert Enoka before his famous All Blacks days because he was a very good friend of Leigh Gibbs, and he'd worked with her in Canterbury netball for a number of years, and with the Silver Ferns for the 1995 World Cup. We asked him to facilitate some team discussions about how they wanted to frame the campaign going forward. The team was selected for the World Champs in about April, and then in May we had a series against England and a series against New Zealand A. Then we went to Miami on the way to Jamaica in July 2003 for the tournament. So Gilbert came into our first series and we talked about our core beliefs. What are the things that you want to be really good at or are really important? He got the girls talking and sent the management out for coffee! They then talked openly about what was important to them and how they felt about being part of the Silver Ferns.

I gather it was Tania Dalton who said, 'When I play, I feel I've got to be a real rock at the back' — and she raised her hand and made a fist —

'because it's really important that when the ball comes down everyone feels that I'm confident to go to the post.' Apparently there was general nodding and consensus, and after further discussion within the team, the rock became our symbol for the World Champs. We extended it in a number of ways. Instead of a Player of the Day Award, it was our Rock Award. So it was like, 'Who's the rock in the team today?' It might have been someone who was on the bench, or who was grounding for the team and helped everyone out. So it acknowledged the values that the team felt were important, rather than just the best player.

The other symbol that was very important for the 2003 team was the kete. Our leadership group charged the team to collect a number of things for their own kete before we went away to the World Champs: items that would connect us to home while we were away. Before the tournament, we were in Miami for eight days or so, so in total we were away for over a month, which was quite a long time for a netball tour. There were a few supporters who travelled to Jamaica, but not many. So we knew that we'd really be on our own over there. In that kete we had to bring a pebble or a small rock from close to where we played our first netball. We had some players from South Africa, so that was a bit hard, but they were charged with bringing something else that linked them back to where they were from in New Zealand. People also placed letters or notes that their family had written to them in their kete, because there wasn't a lot of email access where we were staying. They had little farewell cards that people had written.

We had regular 'sharing sessions' in the 10 days of build-up to the start of the tournament. In our morning meeting, two people (players or management) would share what was in their kete with the rest of the group. They chose what they wanted to talk about, so if anything was really private they didn't have to share. I thought the things that people shared were amazing. We cried lots and lots! We did call ourselves the 'Crying Ferns' for a while, but luckily we finished the 'sharings' before the first day's games!

It was so special having those physical things in my kete when we were in Jamaica. I remember bringing some photos of my children with me, and I often sat on my bed and pulled them out and looked at them. In the end, that's one of the reasons why you play — so that the people who you love can be proud of you as well. That was one of the most memorable things in my coaching life: truly understanding some of those people in the team.

For the 2010 Commonwealth Games, we chose the symbol of the

mountain, because the games were in Delhi and Mt Everest was close by. We started our theme of the mountain quite early on in the campaign. We didn't realise that the Olympic committee were also using it with the whole Commonwealth Games team — especially regarding Sir Edmund Hillary. But in the end it worked well for both our team and the wider New Zealand team. The girls decided that our campaign was like climbing Everest, with different base camps for different netball camps and events. Daneka Wipiiti [now Tuineau] was in the team and she was a very good artist, so she painted an amazing mountain from floor to ceiling. It came with us to Delhi and was centre stage in our team room. As we walked in the door, that was what we saw, and we used it a lot around the symbolism of climbing that mountain, the challenges, and so on.

So these two symbols (the rock and the mountain) were very campaign-related, but the silver fern itself is an amazing symbol for everyone in the team. That whole idea of the respect and the legacy that surrounds it is inspirational and important.

GA

Initially our values and beliefs weren't written down as such, but they were passed on by imitation and discussion. When I was in the team in 1979, we weren't called the Silver Ferns — we were the New Zealand national netball team — but the silver fern was still our logo, our symbol. Lois [Muir, coach] would emphasise the way we needed to play in terms of sportsmanship: to play hard but absolutely in the spirit of the game. So you picked up those values.

The self-responsibility was massive as well, because players are outside the Silver Ferns' environment such a lot. It was about making sure that you were contributing to the team, and also how you were helping to make the team stronger by bringing others on. I was blessed to work in this environment for 10 years and the senior leadership players in that group absolutely lived, ate and breathed those values. If you wanted to be a Silver Fern, then you needed to buy into this. The other value that came through a lot was resilience.

Compared to when I was a Silver Fern, we now have a more formal player induction, and that's the advantage of being in camp. You're in a live-in situation with the Ferns, so while you've got them there, there's plenty of time to do all those other things that are really beneficial.

The most important value that I remember from my coaching time is the idea of 'Silver Fern 24/7': what you are doing when no one is watching. How are you living the Silver Fern values all the time, and not just when you come into camp? You don't just put on a silver fern hat and become a Silver Fern. It's like a cloak that is wrapped around you and a mental approach that stays with you forever.

I remember one of the Ferns saying after the Worlds, when we'd won, that if she went into McDonald's with her children, she felt people were judging her (even if she wasn't eating herself!). I'm aware that people do identify you as a Silver Fern, even when you're in mufti or out of uniform.

Leadership

Leadership is important. Not the 'I'm standing at the front, follow me' kind, but people who are willing to stand up and be counted, take responsibility for the good and the bad. For me as a coach, it was about having the team's back no matter what the result or what challenges we were going through. It was about making sure that I continued to use 'we' and 'us' instead of 'they' and 'them'. When things go wrong, it's easy for a coach to suddenly divorce themselves from the team. It's a little bit like being a parent; you may not like the behaviour or the game play (if it wasn't as good as it should be), but you'll always love the person, even when they get themselves in the most trouble! It's being there through thick and thin, the good times and the bad. It's easy to be a great leader when things are going well, but the biggest challenge is when you're in the pit or in the valley and how you help to get everyone out.

For me, shared leadership is more important than one good leader — I'll have shared leadership any day. It's about growing leadership within the group. Ric Charlesworth [Australian women's field hockey coach] called it a leaderful team — although we never went as far as he did with not having any named captains and everyone rotating. The Silver Ferns captain is out there in the public eye a lot and I don't think New Zealand was quite ready for us to go as far as that. We always had a wider leadership group, though, and we always tried to bring younger ones through.

I'm so proud to see the likes of Laura Langman, Casey Kopua and Maria Folau all coming in at 18 and 19 and seeing their growth and development as people, as much as players, within the Silver Ferns, and them becoming the real leaders six, seven or eight years down the track. It does help if you have good player leadership in a team. If you get people on the same page and you have clear leadership, clear roles, then you've given yourselves the best chance of success.

Leadership, to me, is also about cohesion and ensuring that everyone's on board. If you're a good leader then your empathy should be high. Your understanding or awareness of others within the group — who needs a kind word, who needs a bit of a barrel — that all contributes to the ability of the team to do well and to win.

In terms of coaches and captains, I think that Netball New Zealand does look for people who are good role models and are quite well balanced, because both roles come under intense public scrutiny. So you have to be sure of yourself; not arrogant, but able to deal with challenges and be resilient as well. When they appointed me, it was a big surprise for a lot of people, but I think it was a change of coaching style that they were looking for at that stage. We had a strong group of experienced players, and my strength with facilitation and involving others was the way I think that New Zealand Netball was keen to go. It was a bold decision, and some people didn't think it was going to work. In Jamaica, I took a group of 14 because I hadn't coached many of the squad previously, and I wanted to get to know them better before the selections for Commonwealth Games four months later. We lost to Jamaica in the middle test match, and it was the first time the Silver Ferns had ever lost to Jamaica. I thought I was going to be the shortest-serving coach ever, but I managed to hold on by my fingernails!

GA

As a player in the late 1970s, after we had training camps you got a written review, and you would obviously get feedback throughout the tour and at different times. There wasn't a lot of the one-on-one type of meetings that they tend to run now. There were definitely no individual performance plan (IPP) meetings, no conditioners; you just did your own training. Back in 1979, they sent out a fitness plan and you just did it yourself. Later, when I was coach, the management team and I would sit down with each player and look at their IPP and we would try to help the player drive the areas in which they needed assistance. There was a lot of feedback, but also a lot of personal reflection — much more than happened in the past.

In preparation for the 2003 Worlds, we ran weekly newsletters as the players were spread all across the country and we didn't have the funds for regular camps. I would facilitate this but get others to contribute, just to keep things buzzing along. Nowadays, it's all in the WhatsApp chat group, or something similar, and people are constantly sending things, sharing stuff, quotes, all sorts of things. I used to try to make sure that I got alongside players outside of the one-on-ones that we had through the tours. Also, we tried to meet formally with them to ensure that we understood their goals and they understood what we required. There was often a formal written review at the end of each tour, but it was the informal getting alongside players that was really important.

My coaching style worked particularly well in the Silver Ferns environment over the years, because we had some amazing women. If you don't tap into what these players bring to the group, then you're underselling yourself and the team. I always wanted to help others contribute, including those in the management team. We're lucky enough to have the best in New Zealand in the Silver Ferns management team, and within the playing team, so why not use them? I try to be positive and optimistic. If we are in the pit, it's about finding a way out. I'm a believer in the 'growth mind-set'. It is important to believe that people can do things, and once they believe, they'll succeed.

Emphasis on winning

Winning was massive, as you would expect, but the process is the most important thing to focus on. You have to try to put winning to the side, but it's there — and, yes, it's what everyone judges you by. I remember when we won the 2003 World Champs, for the first time in 16 years. After the final whistle, I felt a sense of relief as coach, rather than euphoria. I think that is probably quite common for coaches. It was a relief that I didn't have to go back to New Zealand and try to defend this wonderful team, because people would have seen us as failures, and I knew different. So to my relief, the rest of New Zealand was able to see them as what they were: strong, dedicated women coming together to chase a dream.

I do remember when I challenged the girls in 2002. We had lost in double overtime to Australia, in Manchester, in the first Commonwealth Games I'd been involved in. I went around the country to sit down with each of the players and look at 'where to from here' for them in terms of looking ahead to the Worlds in 2003. My question to each of them was, 'What are you going to do differently to ensure that, come July 2003,

Silver Ferns coach Ruth Aitken instructs players during the final of the 2007 World Cup. New Zealand lost to Australia 38–42. *Michael Bradley*

we are on the right side of the ledger?' This was my first double-overtime loss, but quite a few of the players had had a number of overtime losses or one-goal losses to Australia in pinnacle events. It had been 16 years since we had won at a World Tournament, so I was pretty honest with them: if we do the same as before, then we will get the same result — second. If we want to be first we have to do something different!

There was a magnificent response to this question, and most players made adjustments to their lives to enable them to train and prepare at the level they needed to perform at their best. In those days there was very little money in the sport and so players relied on jobs to make ends meet. One player took three months' leave, a number moved from full-time to part-time work, and others moved into different home environments to improve their proximity to training and their ability to lead a true performance lifestyle. All of the girls really looked at what they were going to do in their daily lives that was going to allow them to arrive in Jamaica knowing that they were the best they could be. None of it was covered by Netball New Zealand or anyone else; they just did it and used their families, workplaces, whatever they could as support.

In 2010, at the Delhi Commonwealth Games, we had a double-overtime win when Maria [Folau] shot the winning goal. But in 2011 [at the Worlds] we had a single overtime, and a loss. For me, it was really hard because I felt that as coaches, we didn't quite get it right. That will always sit there for me.

Environmental factors

Things certainly changed over the years. It wasn't that I'd say 'jump' and you'd say 'how high?', but in 2003 players questioned things. There was a lot more questioning than when I had been a player. Kiwis in general tend to challenge things and our Ferns also challenge, which is good. They were more confident to challenge coaches and management. The changing nature of the semi-professional environment, once the ANZ Championship came in, also affected the game. In 2003 there was no contract. Players got a bonus when we won, but it was pretty minor. It was purely amateur at that stage. Nothing was driven by money. Today, certainly, there is that other element, the professional athlete. However, I do believe that the change to semi-professionalism is a good one in a lot of ways, because the money allows players to have a more normal life and train at normal times, which has helped keep them in the game for longer.

The media can be challenging, especially when we're not doing well. We do close ranks a bit when we're under siege. We always try to be available and talk to them because they are a part of our sport, and they help us get sponsors and fans. The media tends to only want to interview the experienced players and sometimes it's hard for others in the team. So that is a challenge, but it's also part of what needs to be learnt. We had a rule, that if the sponsor needs to use three of the Ferns in a photo then we tried to get one senior, one middle and one junior, just to keep things balanced.

We have had Silver Ferns continue to train and play in the team when they were pregnant. Often the player will tell the medical and coaching staff, but they usually want it kept confidential from the other players, so they are not treated differently. It is up to the player to decide (with medical support) how long she plays. Silver Fern mothers often return to the team after they have had a baby — but the time frame for this is up to the player. Some come back very quickly and therefore need to bring their baby on tour. The baby will usually be accompanied by a support family member, who stays close to the team. Others wait until their children are old enough to stay at home, and may start back with the Ferns on a shorter tour, as part of the transition. We have had great success with mums returning to play. They have had to make a huge commitment to getting back to the fitness required and they are usually very determined and driven to do well.

Our new mums also love the opportunity for a bit of 'me time' when they come away on tour, so it's the best of both worlds. They get to be a mum and still play top-level netball, and they do it really well. We set the same standards for all the team, but we're a little bit more understanding about the length of time it may take them to get back to full fitness. Netball New Zealand has always been supportive of mothers returning to the Ferns, probably because we've got fewer players than Australia, so we can't afford to lose them! The level of conditioning and the level of recovery is now allowing women to lengthen their playing years, and a lot of women don't want to wait till they have completely finished playing to have children. I remember saying to Graham Henry one time, 'When your chaps come to you and say "we're going to have a baby", you give them leave for three days or so. For mine, that's the whole year.' He just gave me a wry smile.

Jamison
Trophy
NEW WORLD
asics
SILVER FERNS
NETBALL NEW ZEALAND

JULIE SEYMOUR

Julie Seymour (née Dawson) played for the Silver Ferns in 89 test matches between 1994 and 2008. In 1992 she captained the first title-winning New Zealand World Youth Cup team and made the Silver Ferns two years later. She captained the Ferns in 2002, and again in 2008. She competed at three Netball World Championships (1995, 1999 and 2007) and two Commonwealth Games (1998 and 2002).[17]

Julie talks about the immense pride she felt in her selection into the team. She recalls how team values, both formal and informal, revolved around respecting the dress, having a high work ethic and how players represented themselves in public. Speaking about the many characteristics needed in a captain, she notes that being fit, doing her job on court and leading by example were her main priorities. Effective communication between players and with management was considered important, and the inclusion of mini groups of leaders assisted with this — these later became formalised as senior leadership groups under Ruth Aitken. Having played under three coaches and experienced three different approaches to coaching, Julie learnt many different things from each, and she is convinced that this helped her to develop her own coaching style, with a strong belief that no one is a perfect coach.

Australia, she notes, was advantaged in having a bigger pool of players to select from, and their intense work ethic is drilled into them at an early stage. She feels that New Zealand can get left behind in this, and a lack of choice and calibre can affect our selection process. Finally, being one of the first players in the history of the Silver Ferns to have returned to the team after becoming a mum was another major highlight in Julie's career.

I can remember my first series because we played Australia. It was like a baptism by fire . . . I remember thinking this could be the first and last time I play for New Zealand.

Over my time with the Silver Ferns, I found out [about my selection] by different methods, but the very first time I got in, back in 1994, I was teaching at Heretaunga College. It was announced to the media first, and someone rang while I was at school and told me the news. I said, 'Are you sure? Do you want to check that you've got the list right?' It was quite an unbelievable feeling because I really hadn't expected to get in. In those days, with only 10 in the team, it was quite a select few and I guess established players had been dropped. I'm not sure what I taught for the rest of the day; I was on cloud nine, and super excited.

Team culture

Team culture is massive. I'm a big one on culture and the environment. I was in it for a long time, and it was different depending on who the coach was or who was in the team. While at times I thought the culture was stronger than at others, I don't think it ever dipped below a certain line to become unhealthy. Overall, it was still a very positive, strong environment.

Leigh Gibbs was the coach when I was first selected. She had been my Canterbury coach, so in some ways that made the transition easier because I knew Leigh and her style. Perhaps had that not been the case, it would have been scarier. In later years, there was a ceremony that stands out as being pretty special, when one of the more senior players would pass over your dress and welcome you into the team.

I can remember my first series because we played Australia. It was like a baptism by fire, suddenly to be in this team, and I was in the starting line-up, along with a few other newbies. I remember thinking that this could be the first and last time I play for New Zealand. The year before, when Lyn Gunson had been the coach, the team had been walloped by Australia; that was when Netball New Zealand made the change of coach, and then Leigh had brought in some new players. She was a hard trainer, so I knew that it was going to be tough.

Something that stands out for me — I don't know if they do it now — is that on test-match day when you got up in the morning you put on your match kit, and that was quite special. In the days leading up to it you just had your training gear and you never wore your New Zealand tracksuits. I guess, too, we played fewer test matches in a year than they do now, so you might, depending on the year, play only six or seven test matches.

When you're in the team, you're often so immersed in rituals that you don't notice them. It probably changed over time, but that tracksuit thing really struck me when I first came into the team. When I was in the team later, it wasn't a thing that was done so that's something that changed over time. But the ritual of giving out the dress continued in all the years that I was in the team; handing out the kit and the dress.

All the things you do in your game-day walk-through and that kind of thing would be consistent while you had one coach, and then a new coach might come and do things differently. I had three different head coaches in my time with the Silver Ferns — Leigh, Ruth [Aitken] and Yvonne [Willering] — and each had a unique coaching style that brought different things to the team.

Whenever a new coach would come in, you would have values sessions. For me it spanned about 14 years and all the different teams I was in, but often they were about hard work, wearing the fern with pride, valuing the people who had worn the dress before you, and honesty. About what it really means to wear the silver fern, that it's not to be taken lightly, and the dedication that's needed, not just when you're in the team, but when you're away from the team as well. How you represent yourself in public was important because people were always watching you. There was a lot about being a good person. The role models in our team (the senior leaders) ticked a lot of the boxes in terms of demonstrating those values and behaviours both on and off the court.

There were sessions where we would write these values down and keep them in our notebooks. You could be in a World Champs campaign and have a team room and they'd be displayed officially. Different campaigns had different themes. I have memories from when we went to the Manchester Commonwealth Games and the massive team room there.

Family is another big one that stands out. In our team room we had our family wall where we would all have photos of our family or people of importance to us. We had a theme around *The Lord of the Rings*, because that was when the movie came out, and the ring was the gold medal we were trying to win.

Leadership

In most successful environments, I've had strong leadership from all different angles. Not just the captain or a coach: it's got to come from the organisation, the coaching, the management, the senior players. Leadership can provide belief, structure, a pathway and all of those things for players.

To qualify for selection, coaches needed to be experienced people who had achieved success in other campaigns. In my time as a player, first in 1994 and in my last season in 2008, I had only three Silver Ferns coaches; so they weren't changed very often. When I was there, both Leigh and Yvonne got sacked, which was huge. They all had different styles, and they also evolved; the Ruth that first joined as coach in 2001 wasn't the same Ruth in 2009. Netball New Zealand look for coaches willing to adapt and change, and all of them did. There's nothing like being in the hot seat to do all your learning. None of them were ready-made and perfect when they were given the job, but all adapted, changed and grew. This happened with the captains as well; it was all about experience.

And what makes a good captain? I would sum it up as being myself, being supportive, being a good communicator, and having good relationships with the coach and the players. Being that sort of go-between person: feeling that the players could come to me if there were any issues and feeling confident that I could go to the management. Being a kind person, and being someone that the team wanted to listen to; and, ultimately, doing my job the best I could on the court. It's hard to be a good leader if you're not performing on the court when you're a

Julie Seymour and Australia's Natalie von Bertouch (now Bode) scramble for the ball during a test match in Auckland in 2008. New Zealand won 38–31. *Michael Bradley*

captain, so I made sure that I did all my training and got myself fit.

I worked hard and I modelled values such as setting a good example and good behaviours, and also a willingness to talk and communicate, and contribute towards the team, on and off the court. This was important for senior players as well. For example, I wasn't captain in 1999 when we lost the World Champs here in New Zealand, but that's still a lot to deal with as a senior player. When I was captain in 2002, we lost the gold medal match at the Commonwealth Games in Manchester in double overtime. It was tough. On a personal level, you just hit rock bottom, and yet you've got to support everybody else, and face the media.

I was captain on a tour to Jamaica [in 2002] when we had real issues with umpires, and I spoke out in the media against them. I got rapped over the knuckles by Netball New Zealand for that, but that was a tough tour and it was hard to go over there and play. We won the first test and lost the second test, so there was a lot riding on that third test. It was an intense environment knowing that we were going to have one of the umpires who called stepping just about every time the ball entered our third. We had about 30 steps in the game. There were so many ridiculous and different challenges: people getting dropped, sometimes some of your best friends getting dropped from the team; umpiring issues; even travelling overseas. Netballers are lucky in the places that we go, but Jamaica is pretty testing.

The way our communication worked was that we had times where coach, captain and vice-captain went to management meetings, and then other times we'd have player meetings to discuss stuff without the coaches. Sometimes we would all be together discussing stuff. When I was captain, we had subgroups responsible for different areas. There was a strategy group, which I was part of, and a management group, which was more about logistics, and a health and well-being group. That was a pretty good set-up, as it was not just the captain having to deal with everything. There would be leaders within the subgroups as well. At other times, we had senior leadership groups. So rather than having a captain and vice-captain, we had a captain and a leadership group of about four senior players.

Communication was always quite open when I was captain. I can't remember a time when I didn't feel I could say something, and hopefully for players there was a lot of communication going on. The senior leadership group idea came in with Ruth, and it was a formal group in which you were identified.

Head coach was a big role. For Yvonne and Leigh it was the same; they didn't even have an assistant coach. They didn't have someone to chew the fat with or anything like that. When Leigh was first coaching the Silver Ferns she was of the era of 'just knuckle down and work hard, and the harder you train the better'. There were no rest days. It was all about hard work, and it was quite scary. In saying that, I had a lot to do with Leigh over time because she left the Silver Ferns and then came back as assistant coach, and she really changed over her coaching career.

In the beginning, it was a dictatorial type of coaching, very hard and tough. It was a lot about being fit and doing the hard yards, one-on-one defence, and doing the basics well. Then Yvonne came along and it was the complete opposite. There was no emphasis on fitness; with Yvonne it was space-marking defence. Yvonne was a really loyal person: once you were in one of her teams she was very loyal to you.

Ruth was a meticulous planner and — this stands out — a great people person. Her people skills were awesome. She planned every campaign, and if she had areas that she wasn't sure about, she got lots of people in to help. And yet with all those different people, she could plan all that with her amazing people skills. I really enjoyed and learnt so much from all of those people, and now I'm a coach myself I believe that although sometimes as players we look for the perfect coach, there is no such thing. They've all got different strengths. Yvonne's strengths were that base marking and more flair and natural play. When you're in that environment, that's what you pick up on, as well as loyalty to the team. She created a really strong team environment. Leigh would have the fittest team with the best basic skills.

It is important that we have this debate about how much responsibility for performance is on the players. Effective coaching can move a team forward, but you're still limited by the athletes that you have. I've seen teams that don't have effective coaching do really well, so I'm on the fence. I've been in teams where senior players have had a massive impact on a team, the environment, the culture and the winning.

Emphasis on winning

There are too many losses that stand out for me! I was in some humdingers. Any time we beat Australia stands out because, especially in my early years, we didn't play them that often. In fact, for the first few years I was in the team [1995–98], we never beat Australia, but in some of those years we might have played them only once. In 1996 we had three tests against them but only one in 1997. In 1998 there was the Commonwealth Games in Kuala Lumpur and we didn't play them except in the final. Then at the start of 1999 we beat them. So that stands out because it was a big mental thing to have gone four years and never beaten them. I never won a World Champs or a Commonwealth Games gold medal when I was in the team, but beating Australia was pretty special, and the last time I played Australia I won.

Losing to Australia at the Commonwealth Games in 1998 and then probably the 1999 World Champs loss here in Christchurch, my home city, was tough. In 1999 we were winning going into the last quarter and then we lost. Sharelle McMahon shot the winning goal as the full-time whistle went. Kuala Lumpur in 1998 was the first time that netball had been in the Commonwealth Games [New Zealand played Australia in a demonstration game at the 1990 Games — Australia won and no medals were awarded]. Once again, it was another close game. It was goal for goal the whole way until the end when Australia won 42–39. Then there was the loss in 2002, my last Commonwealth Games, in Manchester, England. Those three were devastating moments.

Australia's bigger pool of players means that they have to work hard from a young age to have a shot at playing at top level. We have lots of talented netballers here with lovely skills, but they don't have to work very hard, given that they can get selected for teams because they are talented. In Australia that isn't enough, and the work ethic is drilled into them very early on — because if they don't work hard and they're not fit and dedicated, then someone just like them takes their spot. They're having to work hard and get their skills right from a young age. It would help if we were having to do that at age 12, 13, 14. If you had to drive into every ball that you caught really hard, and mark your player hard all the time, of course your skill level would improve.

There's no way in Aussie you'd make the rep team if you could only run a level 13 on the Yo-Yo [anaerobic fitness test], but we have girls coming into the New Zealand secondary schools team and New Zealand Under 21 team that have poor fitness because they've just never had to work hard, so that's a big factor. Hearing Noelene [Taurua] talking about coaching one of their teams over there, she said the training intensity is 50 per cent higher than when she was at the Magic. They come out on court and train really hard, so they play at that same intensity. We just don't have the practice at playing like that. It's like they're training for a test match all the time, so it's no shock for them, whereas some of our girls will play Australia for the first time and it's a total shock.

Environmental factors

There have been many changes to the structure around the team, and the competition structure is something that stands out. Because the Silver Ferns play so much now, they don't really play at the provincial level, whereas when I was growing up I always went back and played for Canterbury in the NPC, and that was quite a big thing to play for your province.

One of the big changes in the Silver Ferns was the increase from 10 to 12 players. When I was first in the Ferns, with only 10 on the team, you were close to being on the court. You have players now going away with the team that barely get to see the court. The subbing rules have changed, too. When I first made the team you could make only three subs. Now you can put a young player on for five minutes and give them a taste, then sub them off.

The physical side has definitely changed, but because I kept playing for all those years I didn't really notice it. But when I look back at old DVDs, it's changed so much in the number of whistles that the umpire blows. I watched some old games not that long ago and you could have a centre pass and it would go to goal and there would be no whistle. It was amazing. The amount of whistle there is now has completely changed the game because, defensively, people are ridiculous; the things they go for that they're not going to get.

Players also now get more support in terms of nutrition, training and technology — for example, using Power Plates to measure their strength. Then there is the technology around video analysis, which allows the coach to get all your centre pass-offs, all your errors or rebounds, or the times the wing attack, for example, touched the ball. For analysing the game and providing feedback to the players, it is amazing.

Obviously, the payments have changed. During the first part of my career I worked full-time and played for the Silver Ferns, and for the last part of my career I got paid to play for the team — that was my work.

There were major changes with the uniforms. We used to play in the old wrap-around skirts and tops with sleeves that went down to our elbows. The first time we had a capped sleeve, a shorter sleeve, we thought that was amazing. For support staff, we had a physio, manager and head coach, and not much guidance around fitness. A lot of that was left up to the coach. Nowadays it's like having a personal trainer: the girls get people supporting them in the gym for every session. I don't think it's a great thing all of the time, as some of the girls don't have the motivation, or they don't have the knowledge to go out and do a session on their own unless someone's telling them what to do.

I was out for a couple of years while having my kids [see below]. Going back in, I noticed a real difference. I was obviously quite a bit older than some of the other girls, but I felt some of that real love of the game had gone, because they were playing so many more test matches and some of the fun had gone out of it. It was every day, get up, train, come back and rest. When I was first in the team there was a lot more energy to still do all the silly stuff off the court — for example, we had managers who would have dress-up competitions. The mental freshness isn't there because they are playing netball 12 months of the year. We had months and months away from netball, so that when it started up again we were beside ourselves with excitement. Going on tour was so exciting because you only had a couple a year.

I played a series when I was very early in my pregnancy with my first child. There wasn't really anyone else that had done it before. (Irene van Dyk was in the team at the time, but she had to have her baby in South Africa and come to New Zealand and join the Silver Ferns.) At the time, I remember thinking, oh, that's the end of my netball career.

I was sent on one of those coaching courses to start my career in coaching. I went with Ruth Aitken and a couple of other people. Even Netball New Zealand didn't think that I would come back and play, but they wanted to keep me involved in netball in some way. After I had Harrison, and he was a few weeks old, I started running again, and could play netball again. Leigh Gibbs was the coach of the Canterbury Flames, so I started going to their trainings. Then they had an injury and so I came on as an injury replacement. I then got back into the Silver Ferns later that year.

I wouldn't say I played amazingly for the Flames. Then I played for Canterbury for the national tournament. Yvonne rang me up and said, I want you in the Silver Ferns, would you be happy to? I was still breastfeeding because Harrison was only about eight months old, so I said, I'd love to but I want to carry on feeding him. Yvonne said she'd have to speak to Netball New Zealand and get back to me. Then the CEO of Netball New Zealand rang me up and said, we're happy that you bring a support person with you to look after Harrison, but he will not be seen on the same floor as the team and he will not be seen with you at the airport for any media interviews. I got off the phone and burst out crying because I just felt that he wasn't going to be welcomed into the team.

So my mum came on tour. We played against Australia and basically Mum stayed on another floor and I'd go and feed Harrison. I guess Netball New Zealand hadn't been in a situation like that before. I went to the Commonwealth Games in 2002 when Harrison was 18 months old; I got back into the Ferns after Josie, who was my number three. The attitude has changed a lot and other people have had babies go with them on tour, which is great, because you definitely can do it.

There was a lot of media training, especially if you were captain. You'd get advice on how to react to media attention, because at different times, depending on how the team was going, it could be quite negative. You had to not let it get to you. We got pretty good support around mentally dealing with that kind of thing. There are a few netball reporters that aren't my favourite people. It always amazes me that most of them had never played a game of netball in their life and yet they were allowed to write the feature article on the back page of the *Press*, or whatever, about netball. Most of the time it was pretty good, but there were definitely times when it could be negative and affected individuals and the whole team.

Social media, too, is there now to connect fans to the players. The young ones have Instagram and they have followers, and I guess it improves their profile. Therefore sponsors want to get involved with them as individuals — for example, Kayla Cullen or Maria Folau. There's

The attitude has changed a lot and other people have had babies go with them on tour, which is great, because you definitely can do it.

far more opportunity to earn more and have personal sponsorship than we ever had in the early days.

When I first made the team, I felt that we had a good profile in New Zealand. There were good sponsors, and I remember money not being such an issue. We never felt the Silver Ferns were poor or that we couldn't afford to do anything. We had shoes, we had gear, we had everything over time. Economics became more of a topic [in the late 1990s]; we won't be able to do that, we can't afford to do that. So in my earlier years we had some great sponsors. We had things like the Milo invitation teams, so that when the Silver Ferns would be playing [against an international team], the next tier down of players got to play that team as well. That was cool, because that was how I started before I got into the Silver Ferns. I played in the Milo team, and you got to play with other players that were also fringe players.

We also had a North–Central–Southern series when England came. There were teams made up of players who played in the upper North Island, then the central Wellington/Nelson area and then the South Island. So, in all, there were four teams: the three New Zealand teams and England. Yvonne coached one team, Lois [Muir] coached one and Leigh coached another. It was an opportunity for a wide group of players to play with a wide group of coaches. We played in this series with England, and we moved around New Zealand.

Back then, there seemed to be more money for other stuff, whereas now the money goes to the players, and because I'm involved in the

New Zealand Under 21 programme, every bit of money we spend is tight. There's not much spare, so Netball New Zealand has to find that money. Things seem a lot harder now.

I've been through all the different apparel. When I first started we were Adidas, then we went to Canterbury, then we went to Asics, then we went back to Canterbury. So it makes for a lot of gear over the years, that's for sure! We made a lot of TV ads, too; there were the Milo ads and the New World ad. When I was first in the team, we had to do sponsor appearances because of the television coverage. The players were well known around the country, so we had to wear the right gear. But sponsorship contributes positively to the game, obviously, as it brings in revenue, and also some great programmes for players.

In all the teams I've been involved with, it's always a melting pot of different cultures, so it's not something I've ever thought much about. We used to sing the national anthem, but we didn't sing the Māori version, and I can remember — was it about 1999? — that suddenly we were going to be singing the Māori version and having to learn it all. I remember how cool that was.

myob
ANZ

CASEY KOPUA

A long-time player with Waikato Bay of Plenty Magic, Casey Kopua (née Williams) made her debut for the Silver Ferns in 2005, on the end-of-season tour to Jamaica. Earlier that year, she was selected for the New Zealand Under 21 team that won the World Youth Championships at Fort Lauderdale in Florida. She represented New Zealand at four Netball World Cups (2007, 2011, 2015 and 2019) and three Commonwealth Games (2006, 2010 and 2014). Kopua captained the Silver Ferns on 62 occasions, surpassing Lyn Gunson's previous record of 61 tests as captain in 2014. By 2019 she had amassed 112 caps for the Silver Ferns. She temporarily retired from international netball after the 2015 World Cup but made herself available again in 2019 after recovering from a serious knee injury incurred during the previous season.

Casey was made an Officer of the New Zealand Order of Merit for her services to netball in 2011. In her final test she was part of the World Cup-winning Silver Ferns team in 2019, and one of the self-proclaimed, 'fossils' (along with Laura Langman, Maria Folau and Katrina Rore).[18] In an interview, Casey stated: 'Noeline [Taurua] was the biggest reason I came back . . . She instilled this mind-set that we're here to do a job, we're going to do it well and there's no excuses for anything else.'[19]

Speaking on TV One, Noeline highlighted the mantra driving the Silver Ferns at the 2019 netball World Cup: the '100 percent PURE' ethos for her players, an analogy with the New Zealand tourism advertising campaign. The PURE acronym stood for 'Playing to win; being United and ready; Ruthless; and Explosive'.[20] Reflecting on her decision to re-join the team, Casey indicated that '[i]t was totally all worth it. When you've got the belief like that, there's nothing that can stop you. I love my team and my support so much, and I'm so glad that I came back.'[21]

Casey is an advocate of the importance of team culture in any team, at any level. Team values, she explains, are important to have, but it is even more important that the players both develop and fully buy into these values. Leading by example, and having the same expectations for herself as she did her players, were important in her role as captain, and she also learnt what it meant to be a captain both on and off the court. Winning was the priority, and she went into every game with the intention of winning, but it was the process of achieving victory that mattered; that was what players had to think about during the game.

Silver Ferns captain Casey Williams (later Kopua) talks to her teammates during a match against England in London in 2011. *Michael Bradley*

Captaincy is about leading by example. I have the same expectations of myself as I do of anybody else.

The first time [I was selected] was when I got a phone call to say that somebody was injured and could I take their place. It was a total shock, because I'd been to trials, or the camp, and had not made the team. It was my first time trialling, so I never expected to make the team. Then I got a phone call. I thought it was a prank, to be honest!

Team culture

Culture is one of the most important things at Silver Fern level, at ANZ competition level, probably anywhere. If you feel comfortable, you feel safe, but you also feel challenged at the same time, and there's the enjoyment factor. You want to be there, you want to be a part of that group and make the most of it. Also, everybody's heading in the same direction with the same goals. Not everybody has to be best friends and it's not always a box of fluffies, but people need to be able to feel safe, get along and just have each other's backs.

It changes from when you are a newbie to that middle ground, where you move into a bit of a leadership role. I tried to be myself through all of that. You definitely take on different responsibilities, and you're probably more aware of what's going on because you're a lot more involved than when you were a new 17-year-old. So, it definitely changes, but it's not a bad thing: you're upping your role. For the first two years in Magic, I hardly said a word. You're a bit scared and intimidated because you're playing with your idols.

Describing the induction as a ceremony is probably too big a word for it.

But there's definitely a welcoming where you are told how things go, and then you learn along the way. Later, you get a booklet outlining the general behaviours and expectations, and learn more about what it means to be a Silver Fern. When I first made the team, this probably came more from the players. Then, if there was anything on court, that would come from the coaches. The more we got into it, the more we just made it about the whole group. So it's not just 'here's the top and here's the bottom and this is where you are'. It is 'here we all are, this is how we do it and this is how it happens'.

The silver fern on the dress was always the main symbol. For each World Cup or Commonwealth Games, we looked at a different theme and there might have been a symbol for that competition. Sometimes these special symbols were on the World Cup dresses so that the dress was unique. Or it would just be inside the dress, hidden, so only the team would know about it. Before the World Cup in 2015 and the Commonwealth Games before that, we started to have a song that we would sing after each test match in the changing rooms. Everybody does their own individual routine, too.

Back in 2004, the players put together and developed the values and beliefs of the team. That really makes a difference because if you're just given a piece of paper saying 'this is what we do, this is what we stand by', you're not going to get much buy-in from the players. By getting in groups in a room, you get people talking and involved. You get their input, and then you get more buy-in.

Leadership

Back in the day, it was more about the captain, vice-captain and then the coach. Whereas now you have captain, vice-captain and then leadership groups having more input. They're trying not to leave out people who aren't 'leaders'. Everybody is a leader, so what can everybody do to lead or have input? We [senior players, or captain/vice-captain] would be the middle ground for players feeding to us and then we feed it to management.

When I finished playing for the Ferns in 2015, they were trying to have one newish person at every different meeting so they could see how things work, and so they don't get blindsided by what being in the leadership group means. You wanted people to strive, you wanted to be a leader, you wanted to be a part of that group and have input for your team and your culture. We're all here together; whether you're captain, vice-captain or not, you have a role to play for the team.

It's a little different with the Silver Ferns, as you're not together as much and don't play as many games, whereas with the Magic, you're with them every day, day in day out. You're around the team a lot more, so you develop relationships a bit quicker.

Captaincy is more to do with leading by example. I have the same expectations of myself as I do of anybody else, whether they are new, old or whatever. There is leading by example, but also enjoying and having passion for the game. One of my strengths lay in playing the game, but off the court I wasn't so confident. So that was learning for me; to get up and say, hold on a second, I don't agree with that. It is something that grew throughout my leadership as a captain. I'm more a person who wants to get everybody across the line rather than just myself. I can go and play great, but that doesn't mean anything to me. I want everyone else to do well at the same time.

As captain, you are the person who talks to the players and talks to the management, so you can be that middleman, which can be good but also hard at times. You try to please people, but at the end of the day, I just did what was right for our team. I'm not the fittest, fastest person, but I will give 100 per cent on the court. In fitness testing, you can feel a bit inadequate if you're not the fittest. And as you're the captain, you should be the best. Well, that's what I thought: that you need to be at the top of everything. I soon learnt that for me that's not the right answer; it was just to be the best person that I could be for my team.

There is the role off the court as well: sweeping the sheds, making sure the rubbish is picked up, driving the vans, helping anybody out who is in need, but also being able to chill out and have a good time with the girls. You can't be all business and no fun. Everybody needs to feel that you're human, too, because really you're no different to anybody else. Probably the biggest thing is that it is okay to show weakness, to show that you're vulnerable, which is hard. You don't need to feel silly when people see your vulnerable side. They'll be thinking 'she's going through it, too', 'she's only human', and 'it happens to everybody'.

The captaincy also means that you lead the team out on court and you do the coin toss, but once that happens, everybody is equal. It is great if you can get good leadership around you with the other senior players and the younger players. That's something that I've learnt recently: just because they're younger, it doesn't mean they can't teach you stuff, which can be really handy. Once everybody's heading in the same direction and knowing what we're doing and where we're going, it can make a massive difference.

GD

For communication, we used emails, texts and phone calls, but we would also try to meet up on Skype or on a conference call, so everybody was there. Not just players, but at times management too. Leading up to a World Cup or Commonwealth Games, we'd have meetings at the camps. Management would meet without us, but the more time that it's gone on, the more it's come closer together.

Substitutions are always an issue, with people trying to get on court, and some who don't get to play, which is hard. It's a team sport, and everybody wants to get on court. Obviously the players don't get to choose who gets on, so sometimes there's conflict with the coach. Also, there are differences in what individuals want to do off the court. Older ones might just want to relax, while young ones want to go and do stuff and have fun, make the most of their time. That was a juggling act as captain.

As for coaches, they can pull a team together, both on and off the court. But they also read what is happening out on court and make decisions. They know what makes players work, what makes them tick, and how to get the best out of them. Some coaches are direct and know what they want, whereas others are more outside the box. Sometimes we've won with a coach who's out of the box, sometimes with a coach who's very strategic and structured. Some are still learning, as they're fresh to the coaching scene. There are some who don't like to have fun off the court: they just want to coach and they leave the fun to the players; and some you can form a relationship with, not just as a coach.

Julie Fitzgerald [former coach of the Waikato Bay of Plenty Magic] is really good at analysing what she sees right then and there; she knows what to change and how to fix it, and can tell you. Sometimes at the Silver Ferns you're given the same old strategies that might not be working,

Casey Kopua and Katrina Rore defend against Australian goal shoot Caitlin Bassett in the third test of the Constellation Cup in Adelaide, Australia, in 2013. Australia won 58–50. *Michael Bradley*

but you have to do it anyway because that's what you've been told. As a more senior player you develop more relationships, so you can say, I don't think this is working, let's try something else. Most of the time it would be asked in a small group, instead of in front of everybody. Talking in smaller groups was sometimes how you could get ideas and thoughts out of people. Not everybody likes to speak up in front of a group. It's quite hard if you're struggling or don't understand what you need to be doing.

The more confident the coach is, the more you are willing to give something a try. Even if she's told us something and I'm thinking, I'm sure that isn't right, if she says it to you confidently and believes in it, you know you're going to believe in her.

Emphasis on winning

Winning was always the number-one priority. We wanted to win — but in saying that, during the game we were not allowed to, or were trying not to, think about that. We were trying to think about the process of how we get to that outcome. But, certainly, winning is a lot easier than losing!

The travel day, the next day, or with the public and media, things are always a lot better when we're winning. On the other hand, you know that when you do lose, you tend to cover all the bases a bit more: train a bit harder, have a bit more oomph and urgency, because when you're winning you can miss things. That was something we got better at, even when we won. We recognised that there was always more we could do. We wanted to have that winning culture and get into a habit, so that it's not just a one-off win here and there. We were trying to become known for winning, and get people to realise how good it feels and what we could be like. It was just consistency; you need all 12 players to be able to do that, to back it up. You don't have to always play an outstanding game, but we were either hot or cold; we were never consistently good.

[Along with the 2019 World Champs,] the most memorable win for me was at the Commonwealth Games in Delhi in 2010, when we went into double overtime. Australia were fitter than us, but the adrenaline and the passion that we had for the game took over, and there was no doubt that we were going to win. By contrast, losing in Singapore at the World Cup final in 2011 against Australia, again, when we had several opportunities in normal time and overtime to win that game, we were not smart; we did dumb stuff, dumb decision-making.

When I look at Australia sometimes, they don't always play the best netball but they're very consistent, and they hold an above-average performance all the time. It's probably their mental attitude towards everything, their mental toughness. They're fitter across the board, but having a tall shooter helps! They're smarter; they don't throw away that much ball.

Environmental factors

[A decade ago] I used to turn up to training with shoes and a drink bottle, and didn't have to train much at all. Now it's twice a day, every day, because everybody is getting faster and fitter, and everybody thinks bigger and better every year, so that's definitely changed.

I don't have to work; my job is netball. When some of the new kids are moaning about how much they get paid, I tell them, 'I used to get $50 a game in the beginning, so you can be quiet.' The game has become semi-professional. There are more people watching, there's more TV, and there's a Beko team [the development netball league that feeds the ANZ Premiership] underneath as well, so there's more development of the game. Women's sport has grown heaps.

Everybody now is being videoed; there's Sportscode, which is a game analysis program, and GPS. You have to wear a bra over your normal bra with a thing at the back of it so they can read how far you jump — left, right, up, down, everywhere. Everybody is watching everybody pretty much do everything. You can use a phone app to send in your training diary, your logs, your well-being and all that sort of stuff. The new app is cool; our video analysis for Magic can now upload to it, so it's on the phone straight away. We have a Facebook page for our team. It's private so if anybody's got a message or a notice they want to put up there for the team only, then they can.

Media's changed, of course. Before the 1980s you might get one or two games on TV. Netball wasn't so much in the limelight and it wasn't such a 24/7 job. Today, you can't walk up the street without somebody pointing at you, wanting your autograph or photo. Which is cool, because for me it's priceless to have a photo with somebody, to see them smiling. It makes them happy and it's not that hard to do. It's the other side that's tough; when the media are nasty, or they write you off, say that you're going to lose, or just say bad stuff about you. I get protective when people say that about my teammates, but the media are also the ones that put you on the TV, so there are both sides to it. It's about how you want to be portrayed in the public eye.

Before I was captain, I did a little media training, because you can get caught up in the questions that are being asked, and they can make you say stuff that you shouldn't be saying. You're just trying to be yourself, really. With social media you have to be careful what you're doing and who's taking photos of you, but most of the time it's a positive. You can tweet, and be on Instagram, promoting everything.

But you have to earn your stripes. Players have to be realistic. Sponsorship helps because it give us opportunities, it funds us. There is a lot more interest now, with people wanting to sponsor the game. And with all the games on TV, it's huge for netball. You have personal sponsorship as well, which for young players can offer a career or new opportunities. The Waikato Magic team were all sponsored by Cold Power, a washing powder, one year, and a few of us got free washing powder for the whole season.

Now ANZ Premiership teams can have international players, there are opportunities for everybody. At Magic I was the only Pākehā: everybody else was South African, Māori, Cook Island, Samoan, and that's what makes everybody unique — but when you put that all together it's great. The Silver Ferns are not all the same. Somebody would say grace at dinner, and there were different ways of speaking on court. Instead of having just one word — for yelling out 'score', or something like that — we had a Māori word, a South African word; there was something different from each person. We would have cook-offs where people would bring different food from different national cuisines.

It's awesome for mums to be able to play. A male sportsman can still do his job, do something he loves, while his partner is having the baby, whereas for a woman, that's it for you until you get back. It also makes the younger ones and those who don't have babies appreciate the amount of time and effort that a mother puts in. I get a bit angry at people who are late when all they had to organise was themselves!

I only know that because I'm a mum now. A few of the other Magic girls would say, 'I'm so tired I need a sleep,' yet this mum's been up all night. It helps you appreciate mothers, and it's also good for women's sports: it's empowering that women can have a baby, then return to playing a professional sport. Teammates love having the kids around, and if you've got a kid and you can't find a babysitter, you just bring them to practice and somebody will look after them. I was only pregnant for a short while as a Silver Fern, but they supported my decision and my wanting to play; they helped me out. And everybody has supportive husbands, mums and dads, the whole whānau.

A nine-member netball team line up on court, 1920. It wasn't until 1958 that New Zealand switched to the seven-a-side game. *Alexander Turnbull Library, 1/2-000259-G*

PART 5
Legacy

This final section begins by looking back over the development of the Silver Ferns. It charts the emergence of netball, from basketball roots, in New Zealand and how netball became the national game for women. It then focuses on the early interprovincial games and international competition before and after the Second World War.

In the 1970s the name formally changed to netball, Netball New Zealand was formed, and the national team formally became known as the Silver Ferns. By the 1980s netball had begun to embrace increased television coverage and greater commercialisation, but the 1990s were challenging times with no World Cup wins. The millennium saw a change to athlete-centred semi-professionalism and the rise, fall and resurgence of the Silver Ferns, who won the World Cup for the fifth time in 2019.

The final chapter explores factors that have contributed to the Silver Ferns' team culture, leadership and emphasis on winning. There was a consensus from the interviews with coaches and captains that team culture is very important. Initially, it was largely informal, developed and led organically by the senior players, but it became more formalised in the later eras. There were some rites and rituals identified, but these were generally informal and most were used on an inconsistent basis. However, the presentation of the black dress became a formal, consistent ritual, probably the most important throughout the eras. Along with that, the silver fern has always been the most important symbol. And while team values also remained largely informal, three such values were evident and consistent across all three eras: work ethic, pride and behaviour, both on and off the court.

The interviews highlighted two core assumptions that remained unchanged throughout the history of the Silver Ferns: pride in the legacy of the team and in selection, and the acceptance of cultural and personal diversity. Perspectives on winning differed and were very inconsistent, with some emphasising results and others focusing on the processes most likely to lead to peak performance.

Leadership was viewed as being very important, and a shared leadership approach was common. It was demonstrated via both informal and formal means through senior leadership groups, and the role of both coach and captain grew significantly in terms of their leadership responsibilities. Differing coaching styles, ranging from

autocratic to an empowerment approach, affected team culture, with some players responding better to specific styles and not to others. The impact of gender on team culture saw a trend to greater acceptance of players returning to high-performance netball after pregnancy and childbirth.

A 'basketball' match played on the Auckland Domain in 1908.
Netball New Zealand

The development of the Silver Ferns

DR LANA MCCARTHY AND DR GEOFF WATSON

More women play netball than any other sport in New Zealand. It is also among the most watched sports in New Zealand. More New Zealanders watched the 2019 netball World Cup final win than the All Blacks match against Argentina the same weekend, and it was the most viewed news story on the *Stuff* website.[22] Unlike almost any other team sport, netball is a game primarily run by women for women. How and why did this come about? This chapter discusses the development of netball in New Zealand in the wider context of the history of sport in the country. It explains how and why netball became the sport of first choice for women and how it has maintained this position. It also traces the emergence of netball as an international game, and the growing profile of New Zealand's national netball team.[23]

Netball enters our modern sporting world

The sporting world we take for granted today — with regularly organised national and international competitions and clearly defined rules for each code — is relatively recent, dating back to the middle of the nineteenth century. During the second half of the nineteenth century organised sport in its modern form emerged in Victorian Britain and spread throughout the wider world, including New Zealand.

Initially, sport was very much a male activity. Team sports, notably cricket and various forms of football, were actively promoted in Britain's public schools (which, despite their title, were fee-paying and catered mainly for the upper classes). They were seen as a useful means of keeping order among pupils and instilling appropriate 'manly' values, such as acceptance of authority; playing for the good of the team rather than oneself; and developing courage and the ability to play through physical pain. Wanting to keep up the games they had played at school, former pupils devised common rules for the games we now know as football (soccer) and rugby union. By the 1870s, a growing number of middle-class and working-class men, who now had the time and means to play and watch sport, were participating in these games. Many more watched them, leading to the development of enclosed sports grounds and organised sporting competitions played to a regular schedule, such as the Football League (now the Premier League), which began in 1888.

As these competitions developed, so too did the modern professional athlete, although this caused considerable division. Some codes, such as football, cricket and golf, allowed professionalism but ensured it was tightly regulated so as to maintain the dominant position of amateur administrators. Other sports, such as rugby union and the emerging Olympic Movement — the first 'modern Olympics' were held in 1896 — remained the preserve of amateurs. The emergence of the Olympic Movement reflected the rise of international competition between nations in both team and individual sports since the 1870s. Because of its growing appeal among the expanding urban working and middle classes, sport was seen by organisations such as the Young Men's Christian Association (YMCA) as an effective means of promoting Christian virtues among these sectors of society. This philosophy, which became known as 'Muscular Christianity', would play an important role in the development of netball.[24]

The inclusion of women in this new sporting world was a slow process, occurring within a wider context of vigorous campaigning for legal, social and political equality for women during the nineteenth century. The rise of urbanisation in the eighteenth and nineteenth centuries had seen a decline in sporting opportunities for women who had previously taken part in sporting events at seasonal festivals. Such events became infrequent as employers now demanded regular workplace attendance.

Initiatives to increase educational opportunities for women provided the first windows of sporting opportunity in the Victorian era. Advocates argued that it was important for mothers to be well educated so they could better teach their children and be useful companions to their husbands.

This raised concerns among some that women might not be able to handle the physical strain of learning, and that this might affect their ability to bear children. Accordingly, the early pioneers of female education provided for a degree of physical exercise in the growing number of girls' schools that were established in the second half of the nineteenth century. Many pupils proved receptive to exercise and sought opportunities to participate in team sports, just like their male counterparts.

Tennis emerged as one sport deemed suitable for women, because they were expected to play in a 'ladylike' manner and it was one of the very few games in which women and men played alongside each other, enabling prospective spouses to be introduced to each other. During the last quarter of the nineteenth century, some team sports also became available to women. These tended to be either minor sports for men (where female participation was not seen as threatening an established order), such as hockey, or variants of male sports that were specifically developed for women, such as netball. Participation in the football codes was strongly discouraged, because they were seen as too rough for women. By century's end, physical education had been introduced into many boys' and girls' schools. One of the leading figures in this was Martina Bergman-Österberg, who opened a physical training college for women in London in 1885 (it later relocated to Dartford, Kent), and trained over 1300 teachers, who went on to teach throughout Britain and its colonies. [25]

The college would have a significant influence on the global spread of netball. The game arrived circuitously at Dartford via the United States. In 1891 Doctor James Naismith of the YMCA in Springfield, Massachusetts, developed a game to be played indoors during the cold winter months. In particular, he wanted a game that could accommodate varying numbers of players, was easily learned and interesting to players of all ages, and free of roughness.[26] This game became known as basketball and was played by men and women. There are varying accounts of how the game came to the attention of Bergman-Österberg, but it appears to have occurred either in 1895 or 1897. Reportedly, the non-contact nature of the game and its perceived ability to be played in a feminine manner appealed to her and it became part of her curriculum. In 1899 several of her former pupils founded the Ling Association (later renamed the Physical Education Association of Great Britain and Northern Ireland), dedicated to physical education.[27] They printed the first set of official rules for netball to be played by women in Britain. These were later adopted in New Zealand.[28]

The rules allowed variation in team size; teams could comprise five, seven or nine players. The court was divided into three zones, with players restricted to their allotted area so that they did not overexert themselves. The game was restarted by a centre pass after each goal.[29] Until 1970, the game we now know as netball was referred to as 'basketball' in New Zealand and the game we now know as 'basketball' was known as 'indoor basketball'. For the sake of convenience, we will use the term 'netball' in this chapter.[30]

Netball comes to New Zealand

Netball came to New Zealand during the 1890s, a pivotal decade in the development of sport. Sport was becoming more centralised through the establishment of national organisations such as the New Zealand Football Association (1891), New Zealand Rugby Football Union (1892) and New Zealand Cricket Council (1894). The formation of these organisations reflected an increasing number of both domestic and, particularly in the case of rugby union, international fixtures.

The sporting culture of Victorian Britain was transplanted to New Zealand with remarkable rapidity. The earliest interprovincial cricket matches occurred in the 1860s, and the rugby union variant of football came to prominence during the 1870s. During the 1870s team sports tended to be played on an irregular basis; but by the 1890s in men's sport there were regular rugby union and cricket competitions in the main centres and larger towns, alongside fluctuating patterns of participation in smaller centres. Not only was sport played regularly, it was endorsed by leading figures in politics, churches, education and commerce as a health-promoting activity that developed good citizens. It also helped that New Zealand athletes performed well, particularly in rugby union, athletics and tennis.

At a wider level the centralisation of sport reflected a deeper transformation of society. The Liberal Party, who governed between 1891 and 1912, significantly extended the power of government, including establishing the Department of Labour to oversee industrial relations, introducing an old-age pension and granting women the right to vote in 1893.[31]

To what extent were women included in New Zealand's new sporting culture? As in Britain, women had gained a qualified acceptance by the end of the nineteenth century. Discussion on women's participation

Left It is easy to see the origins of the game's original name, basketball, in this photo of schoolgirls playing netball circa 1910. *Alexander Turnbull Library, 1/2-000260-G*

Below A netball match played on grass, circa 1925. *Alexander Turnbull Library, 1/2-028933-G*

in sport occurred within a wider debate around the place of women in society, of which the issue of women's suffrage was the most prominent. Initially women's participation tended to be in individual sports, such as tennis and croquet, that were often played on private grounds. Sport and physical exercise began to feature, albeit to varying degrees, at girls' schools. By the 1880s some schools, such as Otago Girls' High School and Southland Girls' High School, were providing gymnastics.[32] During the 1890s a number of girls' schools played cricket and hockey, with women's hockey clubs becoming established from the middle of the decade.

As in Britain, medical opinion on women's participation in sport was mixed, but there were some important advocates for it. Sir Frederic Truby King, who founded the Plunket Society, believed games were beneficial for women's health.[33] There were, however, constraints. Women's sport was expected to be gentle and avoid physical contact so as not to cause undue strain,[34] so the football codes were seen as off limits. A proposal for a women's rugby team to tour New Zealand in 1891 attracted much criticism, although sports historian Jennifer Curtin noted some newspapers such as *The Tablet* were supportive.[35] Thirty years later, the participation of some women in soccer games and, reportedly, in rugby union and rugby league resulted in a chorus of mostly critical medical opinion.[36]

This was the environment that greeted netball. Exactly when and how the game first came to New Zealand is unclear, but it was certainly present by the late 1890s. References to the early American form of basketball for women, from which netball was derived, appeared in 1896, when Christchurch newspaper the *Star* reprinted an approving article from the *New York Times* which praised the game as 'one of the most excellent promoters of health and spirits possible'.[37] Newspaper reports indicate the game was introduced into Wanganui Girls' High in 1898 and reportedly gained impetus the following year under the direction of a Miss Knapp.[38] By 1914 the game was being played in the main centres and some smaller towns, albeit mostly in schools.[39] It had important allies in the church and education sector and it also became seen as a solution to the problem of providing exercise for the growing number of young urban women. Netball met these expectations because, again, it was non-contact and had designated areas for players which limited their movement.[40] The Reverend J. C. Jamieson, of the Presbyterian Bible Class union, is credited with introducing the game to Auckland in 1906. The first principal of Auckland Teachers' College, Herbert Milnes (principal

1906–16), was an avid netball enthusiast and instilled a love for the game among his students, who later helped to spread the sport to girls' schools throughout the country. He believed it was an 'ideal game' because it could be played in the small playgrounds characteristic of many inner-city schools and could be learnt in 'half an hour'.[41] Bible class teams were particularly important in promoting the game, as the church had an existing infrastructure of facilities and governance experience, as well as conferring moral legitimacy. The Auckland YWCA, for example, promoted netball in 1915 as it 'provides healthy exercise in the open air for girls and develops the spirit of comradeship'.[42]

1919–45: A national game for women

Having established a foothold, netball would become the leading team sport for women in the interwar years. By virtue of its existing support within the education sector, netball was well positioned to benefit from the significant expansion of schooling during that period, which also saw local government provide a substantial increase in sporting facilities in many parts of New Zealand; this, too, worked to the advantage of sports, including netball.[43] By 1925 there were an estimated 183 netball teams in New Zealand, and by 1950 there were 2180 teams (excluding schools) affiliated to the national association (see below).[44] There were, however, continuing constraints. Female sport was seen primarily as an activity for school-aged and single women, as very few married women took part, with some suggesting that their participation in netball was highly discouraged.[45] Hockey remained popular among women, particularly in rural areas, but was not as dominant in urban areas. Netball had the practical advantage that it could be played in a much smaller area than hockey, which made it appealing to many girls' schools that were short of space and, as Ruth Fry has noted, often found their requests for improved sporting facilities for women turned down by school boards.[46] The compact nature of the game also meant it could be accommodated in inner-city spaces, such as the rooftop of the Wellington YWCA. During the interwar period, the majority of courts became asphalt, rather than grass, which allowed games to be played throughout winter without the courts being cut up, but it was a very unforgiving surface if players fell over, and was also hard on players' joints.[47]

The most important spur for the expansion of netball, however, was

Right Women warm up for a netball match on the roof of the YWCA hostel in Boulcott Street, Wellington, 1943. *Alexander Turnbull Library, PAColl-7688-01-03-2*

Below New Zealand's first representative women's basketball (netball) team, 1938. Margaret Matangi (captain) is centre front. *Alexander Turnbull Library, PAColl-0785-1-220-09*

that women enjoyed the game and created opportunities to play at club, provincial and, at the end of the interwar period, international level. The desire to keep playing after leaving school saw the formation of old girls' clubs and workplace teams.[48] Netball proved a popular sport among Māori. The 1931 report of the Director of Native Schools (as schools for Māori were then called) noted the game was 'making great progress' in these schools, thanks to the 'influx of so many trained young women teachers'.[49] In 1939 the South Island Māori Netball Cup, held in Temuka, attracted 400 players and spectators.[50] Margaret Matangi, who captained the first New Zealand netball team in 1938, was of Te Ātiawa and Ngāti Mutunga ancestry and was a sporting Blue at both Victoria and Auckland universities.[51]

Early interprovincial games and the NZBA

The growing number of adult players gave impetus to interprovincial matches. The first official representative match in New Zealand was staged in Wellington in 1923, featuring Wellington and Canterbury. Wellington won the game 24–10. This, in turn, prompted the formation of a national association. In 1924 the New Zealand Basketball Association (NZBBA) was established, adopting the black uniform with a silver fern as the colours for the national team. In 1926 the first national netball tournament was held in Dunedin, with teams representing Auckland, Wellington, Canterbury and North Otago. Tournaments were a standard feature of women's sport in New Zealand because they allowed sporting activity to be concentrated in a week, which made it easier for players to get time off work or school and plan domestic arrangements — which were still largely the domain of women. There was also a social aspect to tournament week, which gave women an opportunity to travel away from home and meet other people. Tournaments were important in promoting women's sport, because they tended to receive extensive media coverage, especially when played in provincial centres.[52] The opportunity to play interprovincial sport was important to players. When the NZBBA cancelled the 1931 tournament, owing to the Great Depression, and proposed to hold tournaments once every two years to save costs, there was considerable protest and the annual tournament was reinstated.[53] Interprovincial games were played as nine-a-side fixtures, but in other parts of New Zealand competitions varied between seven-a-side and nine-a-side.[54]

The new game gained widespread endorsement in the media. In 1926, for example, the *Otago Daily Times* referred to netball as 'a game eminently suitable for every girl, especially the business and industrial girl, who gets practically no exercise during the week'.[55] After the Second World War there were renewed concerns about women's health and the capacity of women to perform the domestic roles expected of them. Again, because it was an avowedly non-contact sport and endorsed by respectable institutions in society, netball was promoted as the ideal sport for females. Moreover, it was increasingly a game run by women for women. Sports historian John Nauright observes that by the 1920s women were becoming more prominent as administrators. The Otago Association of Netball passed an act in the late 1920s stating that only women could occupy positions on their executive, asserting, 'we decided in the end that women should control their own game . . . [the] constitution in Otago . . . cut all men out . . . no male would be appointed to an office'. By 1935 only three of the 31 representatives that attended the annual National Council netball meeting were male.[56]

International competition

New Zealand entered international competition in 1938, when a New Zealand team was invited to the Australian Interstate Netball Tournament. The All Australian Women's Basketball Association (AAWBBA) had been founded in 1927. By 1935 the AAWBBA was eager for international competition and so initiated contact with the NZBBA. In 1937 its president, Edith Hull, attended New Zealand's national tournament and issued an invitation for a New Zealand team to attend the 1938 interstate tournament. There was one significant obstacle: most Australian teams played seven-a-side and New Zealand was reluctant to change. Ultimately, a compromise was reached; New Zealand played one nine-a-side demonstration match, but their other games were seven-a-side matches. New Zealand lost the inaugural test 40–11, struggling to adapt to Australian rules, although they received praise for their 'splendid teamwork'.[57] While 1938 may appear a late starting date for international competition, women's internationals were infrequent in most team sports. After the pioneering tour of 1914, there were no further women's hockey test matches until 1935, and they played only eight test matches prior to 1945. The New Zealand women's cricket team played its first match in 1935 and played only 10 test matches between 1935 and 1961.[58]

Lois Muir takes an intercept during the first test of the 1960 tour to Australia. New Zealand won the match 49–40.
Netball New Zealand

1945–70: Domestic consolidation, international regeneration

New Zealand netball, along with almost all sports, experienced a boom in the two decades following the Second World War. It was a relatively prosperous time which saw many married women re-enter sport, and also the development of suburban sporting facilities.[59] Netball was a major beneficiary of this growth, the number of registered teams increasing from 2180 in 1950 to 4123 in 1965.[60] For all that, though, international netball remained intermittent. In 1948, a decade after the first encounter, New Zealand hosted Australia: all matches on tour were played as seven-a-side games, and Australia won all three tests, plus nine matches played against provincial teams, and one match against a representative Māori team. New Zealand again struggled to adapt to the seven-a-side game, and to the slick teamwork of the Australians, in particular their long one-handed passes.[61]

With New Zealand being the only country to play nine-a-side, its teams were at a disadvantage in international competition and there were increasing calls to adopt the seven-a-side game. These gained added impetus with the formation of the World Federation of Women's Basketball and Netball Associations in 1957, which stipulated international games would be seven-a-side. Some in New Zealand were reluctant to abandon the nine-a-side game, however. There were pragmatic concerns that many more courts would be required to accommodate players and, possibly, a nationalistic attachment to the existing rules. The desire to modernise and play international rules prevailed, and in 1958 New Zealand adopted the seven-a-side game.[62] With four fewer players on court, the new rules made for a much faster game. On the flipside, the reduced number of players per team meant there were now many more netball teams in local competitions and this placed administrators under severe pressure to find sufficient facilities. Manawatū, for example, gained an extra 22 teams in their competition.[63]

New Zealand's tour of Australia in 1960 heralded a move to more regular international competition. Given that no test matches had been played since 1948, the tour represented a new beginning for the national team. They were now playing seven-a-side under the international rules formulated in 1957. New Zealand recorded their maiden victory over Australia when they won the first test 49–40, but lost the next two tests to lose the series. In August 1960 an international body, the Federation of Basketball and Netball, was formed at a meeting in Sri Lanka, along with a revised set of rules, which included the right to intercept goal attempts. It was also resolved that a World Tournament would be held at four-yearly intervals from 1963. Eleven teams attended the first netball World Tournament, which was played at the Chelsea College of Physical Education in Eastbourne, England. The New Zealand team, which included future netball legend Lois Muir, finished runners-up at the tournament. They lost their crucial round-robin match to Australia by one goal, 36–37, setting a precedent for the intense trans-Tasman encounters over the following six decades. In 1967 the New Zealand team won their first international tournament title at the second World Tournament, held in Perth. In 1969 an All Australian team toured, with Australia winning the first test in Wellington and New Zealand the second test in Dunedin.

The advent of international netball stimulated coaching in New Zealand, with the first national coaching school held in Palmerston North in 1965.[64] In many respects, the New Zealand teams of this era created their own culture and legacy, because international competition had been previously so infrequent. The black dress with the silver fern soon became an important team symbol and the core team values of a strong work ethic, acceptance of others and pride in selection came to the fore.[65]

1970–79: Changing name, changing times

The 1970s saw some important changes to the way the game was played. In 1970 the national body approved changing the sport's name from 'basketball' to 'netball' and the name of the national association was changed to the New Zealand Netball Association (NZNA). During that same year, the national playing uniform was also changed, from a tunic (with a silver fern) to a black skirt with a silver fern and a white top. New Zealand remained competitive in international netball, although matches remained irregular. After New Zealand hosted the World Tournament in 1975 a national team was not selected again until 1978. In 1971 the third World Tournament (Championships) was held in Jamaica, with Australia winning the title and New Zealand placing second.[66] In 1975 New Zealand hosted the World Championships for the first time; the tournament was held in Auckland and the home team finished in third place.[67] Skilled diplomacy played no small role in the tournament proceeding. South Africa had not been invited to the 1971 tournament and would not reappear at a World Championships until 1995, but were allowed to participate in the 1975 tournament after both the South African Women's Netball Association and the South African Coloured Women's Association were admitted to the International Federation of Netball Associations (IFNA). This initiative was sufficient to persuade the Citizens Association for Racial Equality (CARE) to call off its proposed protest. The diplomatic approach of the NZNA was in marked contrast to the New Zealand Rugby Football Union (NZRFU), which proceeded with its planned 1976 tour to South Africa and the 1981 South African tour to New Zealand. Unlike rugby union, the NZNA avoided staining its reputation over sporting contact with South Africa and netball remained the dominant sport for women, whereas rugby union ceded popular support to sports like soccer.[68]

By 1976 there were more than 6000 senior teams and 2800 primary-school teams playing netball in New Zealand. Like most sports in New Zealand, netball remained avowedly amateur. Sporting professionals were few and far between and those New Zealanders who did earn a living from sport tended to reside overseas. Like their counterparts in the women's hockey and cricket teams — and men's national teams, too, for that matter — it was taken for granted that being an international netball player, coach or manager was an unpaid position (although public servants were granted paid leave to represent New Zealand).[69] Media coverage was also limited, although Joan Harnett set out to rectify this situation by writing a netball column for the nationally circulated *Truth* newspaper.[70] Players felt that the lack of media exposure meant that the non-netball playing public missed an opportunity to learn about the game.[71] Some saw chauvinistic concerns behind the poor coverage, because the sports media writers were primarily male. There was also a growing tendency for newspapers to focus on particular angles and personalities in sport, whereas they had formerly been content to describe play.[72]

Concerns about the marginalisation of netball reflected, to some degree, wider concerns about discrimination against women. Although the feminist movement in New Zealand, which gained momentum during the 1970s, was primarily concerned with equal wages, child care and women's health, their protests had implications for sport.[73] In 1978 Linda Jones successfully challenged the New Zealand Racing Council's decision to deny her the opportunity to train as an apprentice jockey; she won partly on the grounds that it breached forthcoming legislation on human rights.[74] Women also re-entered the football codes in the 1970s, with women's soccer clubs being formed and a national team playing irregular matches. The first interprovincial rugby match occurred in 1980, signalling the emergence of formally sanctioned women's rugby in New Zealand. Netball, however, remained relatively unaffected by these changes. Geoff Andrew attributes this to its socially sanctioned position as a good sport for women, whose development did not threaten male sporting codes.[75]

1980–89: Embracing television and commercialisation

The 1980s were a transformational decade for netball in New Zealand. Mass television coverage saw the national team and its coach become household names, and commercial sponsorship became part of the game. NZNA president Anne Taylor was a key figure in these developments. During the 1983 World Championships in Singapore she devised the idea of an international netball series, which would be sponsored by Milo, and in 1984 she persuaded the NZNA to actively seek sponsorship. This initiative paid dividends when Nestlé invested $500,000 into the sport and Country Foods Limited obtained sponsorship rights for the national league, which became known as the Swiss Maid League. Lois Muir, the national coach, endorsed this change, stating that 'in sport today you're an entertainer, a promoter'.[76]

Regular television coverage enabled netball to attract sponsors. During the 1980s netball was one of five major sports broadcast on Television New Zealand (TVNZ); the others being rugby union, rugby league, basketball and cricket. Until the entry of TV3 in 1989 there were only two television channels in New Zealand and TVNZ had a virtual monopoly on sport. The influence of television is evident in the NZNA increasing its income from sponsorship from $11,040 in 1982 to $736,014 in 1994.[77] Some believed there was a flipside to this coverage. Nauright argued that some media coverage tended to sexualise players and concentrated specifically on those believed to be the most attractive to men, instead of being based on their level of netball skill.[78] There was also the added pressure of having to win in order to keep the sponsors onside.[79] One further influence of television was a growing trend to move games indoors, so they (and broadcasting) would not be affected by weather. The transition to playing indoors made for a more physical

Margaret Forsyth playing in the 1986 Milo Tri-Series — the first time a major sponsor came on board with the Silver Ferns. *Stuff Limited*

game, because players could contest the ball without risking a nasty fall on asphalt.[80]

The performances of the national team further aided the players' marketability and they became household names. New Zealand shared the 1979 World Championships with Trinidad and Tobago and Australia. In Singapore in 1983, New Zealand lost the final to Australia, although this was redeemed with the famous 1987 World Championships win under the coaching of Lois Muir. The Silver Ferns completely dominated these World Championships, with no other team coming within 10 goals of them. New Zealand also won the World Games, an event for non-Olympic sports, in 1985 and 1989. New Zealand continued their winning streak the same year with a clean sweep of the three-test Milo International Series against Australia. They then went on to win the team award, and Lyn Parker [née Gunson] was awarded the coach/administrator award at the New Zealand Sportsman of the Year Awards. Players of Pacific Island ancestry, such as Rita Fatialofa and Margharet Matenga, made a major contribution to the success of the national teams.

Netball also began to feature in New Zealand's sporting literature. Lois Muir, national coach between 1974 and 1988, was the first New Zealand female sports coach to have a major national profile. Published in 1985, *Lois Muir on Netball*, co-authored with Joseph Romanos, was one of the first commercial publications on netball. Dorothy Simons' 1982 book *New Zealand's Champion Sportswomen* included biographies on Joan Harnett and Lyn Gunson, and Romanos also included a chapter on Muir in his 1987 book on great New Zealand coaches, *Makers of Champions*.[81] In 1989 Muir wrote another guide to netball, aimed at teachers, coaches and players, which included instructions on Kiwi netball, a simplified form of the game introduced in 1988. Like other modified Kiwisport games, it could be played by boys and girls. By 1994 Kiwi Netball New Zealand was looking after 1879 Kiwi netball teams.[82]

From the late 1980s the government assumed an increasingly influential role in sport. The Hillary Commission was formed in 1987 to promote community sport in New Zealand through funding at a grass-roots level via national sports organisations and regional sports trusts. One consequence was the amalgamation of a number of sports with previously separate men's and women's branches, such as cricket, hockey and soccer, because the Hillary Commission would fund only one national entity for each sport.[83] One unintended and unforeseen consequence of these amalgamations was that in both cricket and hockey, coaching female teams was seen as a pathway for male coaches, which has resulted in the majority of men's and women's cricket teams being coached by men.[84] Moreover, because most sports administrators (particularly those in full-time roles) tended to be men, most of the staff of these national sports organisations tended also to be male, so the number of female coaches and administrators declined significantly in both sports.[85] In contrast, netball remained primarily coached and administered by women at all levels of the game, which makes it unusual among New Zealand's major team sports.

1990–99: Rebuilding and rebranding

Like many sports, netball also became more organised and businesslike during the 1990s. The association employed its first executive director in 1989 and changed its name to Netball New Zealand (NNZ) in 1990.[86] The organisation adopted a new logo to symbolise the game — a stylised version of the silver fern — and reverted to an all-black uniform, in a (female) nod to the All Blacks. In formally adopting the name Silver Ferns for the national team in 1991, netball foreshadowed the naming of other national teams, such as the Black Ferns (women's rugby), White Ferns (women's cricket), Tall Ferns (women's basketball) and Football Ferns (women's soccer).

But the 1990s proved a challenging period for the Silver Ferns. The core of the highly successful 1980s teams had retired and it took some time for replacements to emerge. New Zealand was competitive at the beginning of the decade. In the final of the 1991 World Championships held in Sydney, Australia beat New Zealand 53–52 in what many scribes regard as one of netball's greatest games ever.[87] Australia went on to dominate trans-Tasman netball clashes during the 1990s, winning 21 out of the 24 matches played between the teams. The unexpected loss to South Africa during the 1995 World Cup tournament further underscored the difficulties the national team encountered. The decade ended with another heartbreaking loss to Australia in a World Championships when New Zealand, playing at home, lost 41–42 despite taking a six-goal lead into the final quarter.

Australian dominance, however, was one of the few constants in an era of significant sporting change. Men's netball had begun in the 1980s, with the first interprovincial tournament played in 1984 and the New Zealand Men's Netball Association (NZMNA) forming that same year.

The NZMNA amalgamated with Netball New Zealand in 1996. Men's netball, however, remained a minor pursuit, with only 50–60 teams affiliated to Netball New Zealand in 1994, although there were some social mixed netball competitions played outside NNZ's jurisdiction.[88] It was not until 2019, when the New Zealand men's team won a Quad Series against the Silver Ferns, an All-Star Team and Fiji, that a men's game was broadcast on prime-time free-to-air television.[89]

The corporate appeal of netball was reflected in further sponsorships from major businesses. In 1996 Fisher & Paykel Appliances became the major sponsor of NNZ and the Silver Ferns, along with the introduction of the Fisher & Paykel Cup for annual trans-Tasman clashes. Franchise competitions, which had been popularised in New Zealand with the introduction of Super Rugby in 1996, were introduced to netball in 1998 when the Coca-Cola Cup was revamped from a club competition to an elite regional franchise competition.[90] The competition was run on a semi-professional basis, with some elite players being well rewarded for their services. The Southern Sting, based in Invercargill, dominated the competition, winning the title on seven out of the 10 occasions it was contested and making the final in the other three. They introduced a new era of professionalism into netball in New Zealand, flying Auckland-based players Tania Dalton and Bernice Mene to Invercargill to play for the team and attracting massive support from their local community. Most players in the Coca-Cola Cup, however, received minimal compensation. The maximum signing-on fee at the beginning of the competition was $250 and match fees were limited to $50 per match. So players received around $1500 per season. In contrast, a Super Rugby player in 2002 received a minimum $65,000.[91]

Therefore, the introduction of player payments did not allow most competitors to be professional sportswomen. They still worked or studied, since being paid to play netball could be cut short at any moment via injury or deselection. Some netballers, like Adine Wilson, also benefited from Prime Minister's Scholarships.[92] In addition to the development of the domestic game, the international game received a major boost in profile when netball became a Commonwealth Games medal sport for the first time in Kuala Lumpur, Malaysia, in 1998. The Silver Ferns won the silver medal after losing to Australia in the final.

Despite a poor run for the Silver Ferns, public support continued. Maintaining a strong public profile for netball was increasingly important, too, because women now had a much greater range of options when it came to playing and watching sport. The emergence of women's rugby (in particular the women's Rugby World Cup), the growing number of women playing soccer and the White Ferns' Cricket World Cup win in 1999 challenged netball's previously dominant position. Accordingly, any offer of media exposure was generally accepted to ensure netball's promotion. Media demands began to increase, with both pre- and post-match interviews taking place, particularly with coaches and captains.[93] Viewing figures of over one million for the 1999 Netball World Cup final, the highest-rating programme ever at the time, testified to the sport's enduring popularity.[94] Electronic technology also became more common in the game, with players and coaches using video analysis to review their own matches and those of opponents.

The 1990s culminated in the seventy-fifth anniversary celebrations for Netball New Zealand. The 1999 annual awards neatly encapsulated the trajectory of netball. There was a nod to the past, with long-serving personalities such as Lois Muir, Anne Taylor and Dawn Jones receiving awards. The event itself, however, was sponsored by Vodafone, a major corporate sponsor whose support underlined the commercial value of the game. A 'dream team' of past and present players was also selected: Margharet Matenga, goal shoot; Joan Harnett-Kindley, goal attack; Rita Fatialofa, wing attack; Sandra Edge, centre; Lyn Gunson, wing defence; Yvonne Willering, goal defence; Tracey Fear, goal keep. This dream team concept was a common practice amongst male sports and the naming of a Silver Ferns equivalent represented a desire to formally honour their history.[95]

2000–19: Athlete-centred semi-professionalism

The noughties saw netball transition to semi-professionalism for franchise players and full professionalism for an even more elite group. After the conclusion of the National Bank Cup (a semi-professional domestic competition) in 2007, the trans-Tasman ANZ Championship began the following year.[96] Initially, netball increased in popularity and media coverage expanded, with the sport bringing in more sponsorship dollars than ever. New Zealand teams, however, struggled against their Australian counterparts in the competition, the Bay of Plenty Magic in 2012 being the only local team to win the competition. The performance of

Bay of Plenty Magic's Monica Falkner and Mainland Tactix's Zoe Walker in action during an ANZ Premiership match in Hamilton in 2017. *Michael Bradley*

New Zealand teams relative to their Australian counterparts would remain a major point of contention. Australian netball personalities argued that their own deeper talent pool justified more teams. The final breaking point came with changes to the format in 2015, which, according to Australian netball enthusiasts, tilted the competition in New Zealand's favour with the introduction of the two separate conferences guaranteeing two New Zealand franchises entry into the semi-finals. Netball commentator Sue Gaudion believed the changes were 'a slap in the face' for all Australian teams, who battled hard all season only to then see 'less deserving New Zealand sides' make the finals.[97] The ANZ Championship formally ended in 2016.

The end of the nine-year trans-Tasman partnership saw both Australia and New Zealand move back to standalone domestic competitions, with the ANZ Premiership revealed as New Zealand's new national league. However, there were concerns expressed by fans who feared that the lack of contact with the Australian teams would result in a steep decline in Netball New Zealand's competitive standards and would lessen the competitiveness of New Zealand teams.[98] NNZ also decreed that only players who played in New Zealand competitions would be eligible for the Silver Ferns, a decision that rendered one of the Silver Ferns' best players, Laura Langman, ineligible for the 2018 Commonwealth Games, given that she played for the Sunshine Coast Lightning.

The advent of professionalism had both costs and benefits. Some coaches were concerned that professionalism was a disincentive for some fringe players to move franchise and seek more game time because they were content to simply be paid for being in a professional netball team.[99] Such concerns, however, need qualification. Although some players were able to earn a living from the game, their incomes remain modest compared to other codes. The Silver Ferns are on annual four-tiered contracts, which begin at $20,000–45,000, with match payments of $1500 per test added on top. Leading Silver Ferns players can earn more than $130,000 a year, including their domestic contracts, with some also having their own personal sponsorship and endorsement deals. For franchise-only netball players, the top end of the salary scale is $60,000–80,000, with a minimum contract of $22,500.[100] It was only after a public outcry that the victorious 2019 World Cup-winning New Zealand team was collectively awarded a $300,000 bonus ($25,000 per player).[101] By comparison, in New Zealand's second-tier rugby competition, the ITM Cup, the maximum provincial rugby salary is set at $55,000 over an

11-week period and the New Zealand men's cricket team received a prize pool of $3 million after finishing runners-up in the 2019 Cricket World Cup.[102] Despite receiving some payment, few netball players can rely solely on netball to cover their living costs, so the need to fit netball around seasonal or part-time work is crucial.

The emergence of social media has also presented both opportunities and challenges. On the one hand, it serves as a connection to fans, helps to improve the individual reputations of players, and helps to entice sponsors for individuals, which increases revenue for players. On the other hand, players have to be careful and a lot more aware of their actions.[103]

The ability of NNZ to secure sponsorships and income from subscriber television is due in no small part to the loyalty of the netball fans who have continued to support the game. Netball has retained a high profile in the media in New Zealand, with live test matches on subscriber television and live coverage of national league games. This makes New Zealand something of an outlier when it comes to supporting women's sport. Sports journalist Dana Johannsen observed that 'New Zealand is the only country in the world where a women's sport sits alongside men's sport in television ratings'.[104] Administrators are conscious of the importance of maintaining public support. Players, coaches and managers are provided with media training, which is particularly important for national representatives. One of the main reasons for netball retaining its status as the leading team sport for women is that it has always maintained a positive image in the media. In contrast to other codes, players have been largely free of off-field scandals and are widely regarded as positive role models.

The culture of New Zealand's high-performance female sports teams has been the subject of scrutiny, with reviews of the Black Sticks women's hockey team and the Football Ferns in 2018 highlighting concerns about the team environment and player welfare.[105] Although there was a performance-related review of the Silver Ferns following their fourth placing at the Commonwealth Games, there have been no reports of mistreatment of players. This may reflect netball's position as a game largely run and coached by women. Certainly support and engagement remain high in the community game. Netball New Zealand's 2018 annual report stated there were 139,529 registered players; 3.2 million viewers had watched the game on television; and they were the second-biggest sports brand in New Zealand with 307,489 social media followers.[106] Netball New Zealand also has a wide range of corporate sponsors.[107]

While netball has seldom been linked explicitly with the feminist movement, there has been a growing trend towards elite players combining motherhood with their playing career. This owes much to a marked change in attitudes. In previous eras players felt their babies were not welcomed in a team environment; there remained no financial or other support for new mothers, and they were expected to provide their own support person to attend trainings and games, to assist with the baby at their own expense.[108] By the late 1990s, however, there was some support for new mothers (albeit not financial), with a more welcoming team environment helping them feel that they could return to playing netball after giving birth. Nonetheless, there was still the same expectation placed on returning players to be fit and capable of playing at an elite level.[109] More recently there has been a growing acceptance that women could play at an elite level while pregnant and later, as mothers, return to national-level sport. Within the Silver Ferns squads there was an increase in the number of players becoming pregnant or being available for selection after a pregnancy. While this did pose a challenge at times for the coaches, for players to able to have a baby and then return to the Silver Ferns was regarded as being very special and empowering. It was also identified as a point of difference between male and female high-performance sport.[110]

2000–19: Rise, fall and resurgence

From an international perspective, the first decade of the twenty-first century saw a resurgence of the Silver Ferns. They won the World Championships in 2003; their first title since 1987. The following year, they dominated the New Zealand Sports Awards, winning the Halberg Supreme Award, with Ruth Aitken named Coach of the Year and Irene van Dyk awarded Sportswoman of the Year. In 2005 they achieved their largest winning score against Australia with a 61–36 result in Auckland. The following year the Silver Ferns headed to the Commonwealth Games and won the gold medal for the very first time with a 60–55 win over Australia in the final in Melbourne.[111] They defended this title in Delhi in 2010, winning 66–64 in overtime. One factor in New Zealand's resurgence was the selection of players who had previously resided in South Africa and had resettled in New Zealand, notably star shooter Irene van Dyk and defender Leana de Bruin (née du Plooy). New Zealand also proved adept at the new Fast5 format, winning the title in 2009 and 2010 and winning seven out of nine tournaments played through to 2018.

But if the first decade of the century was a relatively successful era, the second has seen major fluctuations in performance. Australia reasserted their dominance in the World Championships, winning the 2007, 2011 and 2015 tournaments. The Silver Ferns had occasional moments of success, winning the inaugural Quad Series competition between New Zealand, Australia, South Africa and England, and the Constellation Cup (a new competition between New Zealand and Australia initiated in 2010) in 2012 for the first time.[112] Janine Southby began her new role as Silver Ferns head coach in 2016. Initially, the team had some successes, winning the Quad Series in 2017, following an emphatic defeat of Australia in Invercargill. Unfortunately, the team's performances declined from that point. New Zealand lost all four matches against Australia in the 2017 Constellation Cup and had a disastrous Commonwealth Games in 2018, losing to Malawi in group play and missing out on playing in a Commonwealth Games final for the first time after they lost their semi-final against Jamaica.

This disappointing loss prompted an independent review conducted by an autonomous panel, which produced the following key findings. During 2016 and 2017, the team had 'lost a vast amount of experience through the retirements of key players', losing both talent and core leaders; only three of the 12 players had gone to the previous Commonwealth Games in 2014; and 'for eight of the 12 this was their first ever pinnacle event'. Also, both coaches were 'relatively inexperienced at international level' and were found to have similar skills yet were determined to be 'too similar' and lacked 'complementary skill sets'. The head coach, the panel concluded, was 'committed to developing a player-led culture', expecting players to take ownership of their decisions. 'Unfortunately,' however, 'that philosophy did not connect with the team.' The findings also showed that several players began to 'lose confidence in both themselves and the coaches during the course of 2017', taking this lack of confidence into the 2018 netball season.

The review also identified some underlying issues in the national game, asserting that netball in New Zealand struggled to 'embrace a true high-performance culture' that eschewed 'shortcuts', and it advocated for more investment in the high-performance programme and more netball expertise on the board of Netball New Zealand.[113] In mitigation, it must be acknowledged that Southby was unable to select Laura Langman, owing to the eligibility criteria adopted by Netball New Zealand in 2016.

Left Silver Ferns coach Janine Southby with the team in a half-time huddle during a match against the England Roses in Liverpool, 2017. New Zealand won 61–37.
Michael Bradley

Left Janine Southby coached the Silver Ferns at the 2018 Commonwealth Games, where New Zealand lost to Malawi for the first time in its history (53–57). Southby resigned after a review into the team's disappointing performance at the games.
Michael Bradley

The findings of this review resulted in Southby's resignation; contracted to fulfil her head coach role until the World Championships in June 2019, she was replaced by Noeline Taurua, who had prior experience as an assistant coach of the Silver Ferns under Ruth Aitken in 2011. Taurua also had great success as head coach of the Waikato Bay of Plenty Magic ANZ franchise (winning the title in 2012), and latterly as head coach of the Australian franchise team the Sunshine Coast Lightning, which won the Australian National Netball league in 2017 and 2018. Netball New Zealand revised its eligibility policies, allowing Langman, who played under Taurua for the Lightning, to be reselected. Casey Kopua, who had retired after the 2015 World Championships, also declared herself available for selection. The change of coach did not result in an immediate return to winning form, with only three wins in the first 10 games. By the time of the 2019 World Cup, however, the Silver Ferns were in peak form, losing only once to Australia in their eight games. As coach, Noeline Taurua placed a major emphasis on fitness, with some players being ruled ineligible for selection for missing the required fitness levels. The reintegration of experienced players Kopua and Langman, along with the high levels of fitness and self-belief Taurua instilled in the team, were leading factors in the 52–51 victory over Australia in the World Cup final.

Conclusion

Netball has seen many changes in the more than 120 years it has been played in New Zealand. Initially a non-contact game designed to restrict player movement so as not to exhaust its participants, it has evolved into a sport that demands uncompromising fitness, and the modern-day netballer is an athlete on par with any other. For many years an avowedly amateur game, netball now commands extensive support from the corporate sector, and its players, administrators and coaches are articulate spokespeople for their game and much in demand from sponsors. Although the rewards are modest compared to other codes, it is nevertheless possible to earn a living wage playing netball and for leading players to leverage their profile via social media. For all the changes to the form of the game, it has retained its core character as a game primarily played and administered by women. The pride in wearing the black dress and representing New Zealand has also remained constant throughout the history of the national team.

Team culture, leadership and the emphasis on winning

DR LANA MCCARTHY, DR ANDY MARTIN AND DR DENNIS SLADE

This book set out to examine the importance of team culture, leadership and the emphasis on winning within the Silver Ferns, and to investigate how and why this has changed over time. This chapter draws together research on team culture and the perspectives of interviewees and identifies some broad conclusions. This study is informed by the theoretical framework of Schein's three-level model of organisational culture, using artefacts (rites, rituals and symbols), values and beliefs, and core assumptions.[114]

Team culture

The importance of team culture was identified as a significant theme for the Silver Ferns. The development of this team culture is founded on pride in selection and being a Silver Fern, and the welcoming and embracing of all players when they enter the team. The time spent together as a team off the netball court was identified as another significant impact upon team culture.

A variety of views were expressed about how the team culture was developed over the three eras. One perspective was that culture developed through using a collective approach, where individuals put the team first and worked together towards achieving a common goal. However, others perceived the culture was largely led and influenced by the coach and senior leaders of the team. It began with no 'formal' approach to developing team culture, being largely determined by the coach in the first era. The second and third eras both saw a change, with the senior members largely creating the culture by passing it down to the newer, younger players, who were expected to fit in. Some interviewees believed this influence created a 'hierarchical' effect, impacted by those who were in charge at the time. Others felt having a 'consistent' coach and/or a stable group of senior leaders made creating and upholding the team culture far easier. It was also perceived that a loss of these senior players resulted in a less effective team culture, and the team was less cohesive.[115]

Throughout all eras, aspects of Schein's three levels of organisational culture are evident, albeit some more so than others at times. Culture and team leadership are promoted and created through change, based on the mutuality and collaboration of the players in the team at the time. Developing a team culture through bringing people together from diverse backgrounds, creating relationships with one another, encourages working towards a shared goal or purpose. Figure 1 presents a model for developing the Silver Ferns' team culture based on the findings of this current research, which clearly identifies the roles and responsibilities of team members and outlines the implicit and explicit expectations of being a Silver Fern.[116]

- Core assumptions — pride in the selection, legacy and representing New Zealand in netball
- Collective culture — acceptance of all players from various ethnic and cultural backgrounds
- Symbols — the black dress with the silver fern
- Rites and rituals — the presentation of the black dress as an artefact that helps reinforce the values and core assumptions
- Values — work ethic, pride, behaviour on/off the court
- Leadership — the importance of the role of coach and captain in demonstrating leadership, and a mixed-methods approach to coaching styles combining both autocratic and empowerment styles

Our research endorses Schein's theory of organisational culture involving the use of artefacts and creations, rites and rituals, values, and core assumptions. The findings show the importance of both team and individual rituals, explicit values, pride in the fern and the black dress as team symbols, the importance of effective leadership, core assumptions

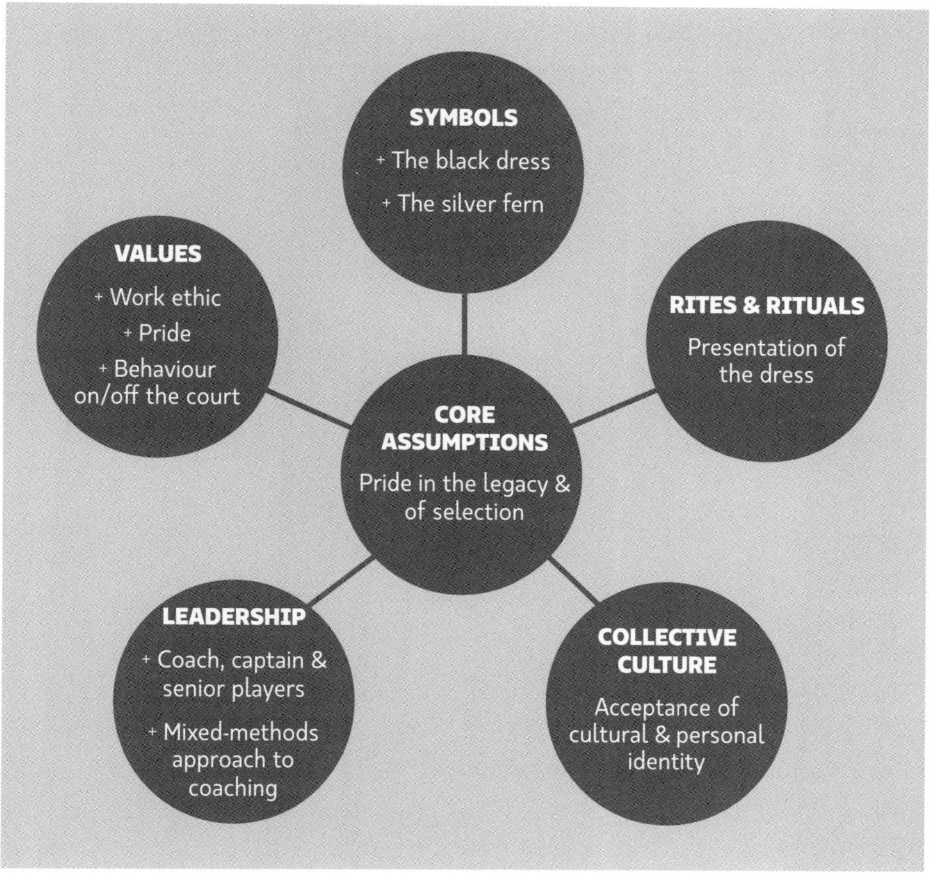

Figure 1 Model for developing a successful Silver Ferns team culture. *Adapted from Johnson et al., 2014*

around cultural diversity, and pride in the legacy and selection. All these aspects, involving the coach, captain and senior players, are linked to creating a team culture.

INDUCTION

The first era (1960–87) saw no formal induction of new players when they first made the team. Once selected, they had to immediately accept and demonstrate the behaviours already established by the senior team members. This included expectations regarding their commitment and work ethic at training, and putting the team first. This informal process continued in the beginning of the second era (1988–2001) but began to change when Leigh Gibbs became coach in 1994: it became slightly more formalised, with the inclusion of some rituals, such as being presented with a player handbook and the playing uniform by a senior player. This process was still not considered consistent, with some players inducted in this manner and others not. The final era saw a much more consistent formal induction process for new players, still upholding many of the rituals established in the previous era, but on a more regular basis.

RITES AND RITUALS

There was a lack of consistent, formal rituals, particularly up to 1994. Some initial rituals, such as singing team songs, performing a women's haka and singing waiata, were evident. There were both team and individual rituals in all three eras that were considered important, including the wearing of particular clothing, certain pre-game warm-up exercises, and post-match songs. The most significant ritual involved the senior players presenting the black playing dress to the new team members as part of their induction into the team, and to recognise the honour of being a Silver Fern. This ritual was considered special and was upheld throughout the second and third eras.

SYMBOLS

There were several different tangible symbols identified across the three eras. In the first era, a Māori doll served as the team symbol, while the third era saw the kete and specific themes as the main symbols associated with various netball tournaments. The concept of a specific 'theme' for various campaigns continued throughout the third era, with the symbol for that theme sewn on the inside of the players' black dresses. The rock was another key team symbol early on in the third era (2002–19). The most significant symbol across all three eras has been the silver fern, which was formally adopted as the symbol and name for the national team in 1991. All of the interviewees expressed an immense amount of pride in wearing the black dress with the silver fern.

VALUES

During the first era, team values were not discussed in a formal team setting and were unwritten. Through a more informal process, the coach and the senior members modelled these values to new players, who were expected to accept and adopt them. Creating team values became slightly more formal in the second era as they were discussed within the team,

Right From left: Maria Folau, Julie Seymour and Adine Wilson. The most significant symbol across the decades has been the silver fern, which was formally adopted as the name for the national team in 1991. *Michael Bradley*

Below Pre- and post-match rituals, such as the team huddle, are an important factor in the culture of the Silver Ferns. *Michael Bradley*

although still not written down, but continued to be modelled by the senior players and passed down. In the third era, team values remained extremely important, but there was still a hesitancy to write them down in a formal manner, due to the difficulty of gaining player buy-in. Indeed, one contributor felt that not all players demonstrated these team values on a consistent basis, both on and off the court.

Three significant values identified by the interviewees have been a constant throughout all three eras. They were work ethic, pride and good behaviour. Again, these were not written down, but rather demonstrated. A strong work ethic was an essential value in being a Silver Fern; it was the responsibility and expectation of all players to demonstrate this value, both as individuals and as a team. Pride was hugely important and identified as being part of the legacy of the Silver Ferns. Players took pride in selection, in their performance and in wearing the fern. Good behaviour was the third consistent value identified, and it applied both on and off the court.

CORE ASSUMPTIONS

Two main core assumptions were unchanged across all three eras and were accepted as the norm by those who became a Silver Fern. The first was the pride in being named a Silver Fern and its associated legacy. Creating and then sustaining the legacy and pride became a significant part of the team culture. A second core assumption was acceptance of players from different cultural backgrounds and with different personalities. All cultures were acknowledged, appreciated, respected and incorporated in different ways. For example, speaking different languages on court, and team cook-offs in which players cooked food from different countries. Māori culture in particular was always strongly recognised throughout all three eras, through the singing of waiata, a karakia at team dinners, and, more recently, singing the national anthem in both English and Māori. Although cultural acceptance was a significant core assumption, it was identified across all three eras that everyone was in fact 'the same'; they were there for one purpose, to play netball.

Leadership

Interviewees considered leadership to be very important through all three eras, and necessary in order for everyone to work together towards a shared goal. It was identified in the first era that having a stable core group of players and coach was an important factor, but that all the members of the team played key roles too. All team members worked informally, yet cohesively, to demonstrate leadership, without it being considered solely the captain's responsibility. From the first era into the start of the second, leadership remained crucial and important, yet there was no formal training on how to be a leader. The necessity of a solid core of experienced players leading the group was still noted in the second era, and interviewees linked it to the team's successes.

The introduction and recognition of leadership groups first arose at the beginning of the second era, when senior members of the team informally took on leadership roles as a way of helping the captain and the coach. In the latter part of the era (when Leigh Gibbs was coach) there was an attempt to establish leadership groups using a more formal approach. However, the coaches felt this was met with some criticism, due to a lack of understanding by the players and media about what the coaching team were trying to achieve. It might also be argued, as will be discussed later, that the coaches were ahead of their time in implementing this approach, which then became common practice. During this time, the coaching and management group also implemented a 'collective' leadership approach that included using specific terminology such as the word 'team', with the intention of creating a 'leaderful' team where everyone had buy-in. The coaching staff believed everyone needed to be a leader at some point, and therefore a more collective approach towards leadership emerged.

In the final era, leadership within the team was seen as being as important as ever. The collective approach towards leadership that was initiated by Ruth Aitken was still the preferred approach in the early stages of this era. The more formal leadership groups were still evident, although leadership tended to be demonstrated by all players in their own individual ways, and even those not specifically included in this leadership group were still considered as leaders.

LEADERSHIP BY COACHES

Coaches in the first era demonstrated leadership by respecting players equally, making the best decisions for the team regarding players and court time, and ensuring effective two-way communication with players and management. Many of the qualities a coach was perceived to need in order to effectively demonstrate leadership were consistently expressed across all eras, including respect and care for others, effective communication and decision-making skills. It was also a common view of the coaching team to present a united front and that all needed to be on the same page when it came to coaching and making decisions. However, the substantial increase in publicity and media requirements in the third era placed increased pressure on the coaches. They now had to lead and act confidently in the public eye, show resilience, have the ability to sell netball as a 'product', and generate sponsorship and income.

LEADERSHIP BY CAPTAINS

As captains, the interviewees identified specific qualities they were expected to possess in order to demonstrate effective leadership. Across the three eras these were: consistent performances on court; demonstrating respect for others and being respected by the coach, management and teammates; being a positive role model to others in the team, leading by example both on and off the court; demonstrating effective communication; and always appreciating team members and their differences. Until the third era, the captains had to do all of this without being offered any formal training on how to be a leader. Due to the changing environment, some new qualities were identified in the third era that differed from those in the previous two. Specifically, captains were now expected to possess even better communication skills due to the increase in public speaking and media responsibilities.

Coaching leadership and styles

During the first era, coaching styles were a mixture of autocratic and empowering approaches. Coaches instructed players in terms of their training focus, but there were also signs, during Lois Muir's time as coach, of an empowering athlete-centred approach being implemented, seemingly well before its time, as a style widely known to be effective. Coaches wanted to create 'thinking' players who could make decisions on the court under pressure, when it really mattered. It was considered important by coaches that they instil personal belief in players so that they became capable of taking ownership of their own performance. Coaches stressed the importance of accepting players for their own natural abilities and that everyone brought with them their own different skills. They believed that this approach made players feel supported and welcomed within the team.

Lois Muir, Silver Ferns coach from 1974 to 1988, admits she was sometimes hard on the players, but her approach earned their respect. *Photosport*

It was clear that the coaches were very highly respected despite the more authoritarian coaching style that was being used at the time. Lois Muir described herself as being 'mean', with limited praise given to players, yet was described as being very well respected and adored by her players, even though she was hard on them. There was a significant shift in coaching style in the second era, with the empowering approach much more dominant, particularly under Leigh Gibbs (1994–97). However, it was thought of as being before its time, and less effective than Gibbs had envisioned, with the players preferring a mixture of coaching approaches as they felt this was much better in developing them into well-rounded players with a range of skills.

The final era saw the coaches implementing different coaching styles, beginning with the continuation of the empowerment approach from the previous era. Successive coaches then utilised both autocratic and empowering styles of coaching to different degrees. The present coach, Noeline Taurua, is known for being very clear in her expectations of players.

A certain style of coaching and the receptiveness of the players to that approach are very much part of establishing a strong team culture. The research on coaching styles for the Silver Ferns (from 1960 to 2019) did not reveal any one preferred method of coaching. What was revealed was that coaching practice tended to mirror mainstream educational and teaching pedagogy, and that eventually a combination of styles emerged based on player expectations and coach philosophy.

FIRST ERA (1960–87)

Of this era, it could be said that initially the style of the Silver Ferns' coaching reflected New Zealand's sociocultural legacy of the recent historic past, in that it was tied to our experiences in the Second World War. Society was accustomed to regimentation, with a hierarchy of people giving orders. Indeed, it emerged from the interviews that in this era there was a two-way expectation: the players looked for that approach from the coach, who in turn was under pressure to deliver on that expectation to the players and the public. The person appointed to coach, the person who selected the players, was perceived as all-knowing in matters netball. Coaches in this era were autocratic and command-based, and teams were solely coach-driven.[117] The coach was responsible for all aspects of the sessions that covered all aspects of play. There were no assistant coaches, and while player initiative no doubt manifested itself at times on court, in game preparation there was little expectation from the players on the coach to seek such input, nor was it anticipated from the coach that players expected them to provide opportunities for collaborative input.

In recognising this style of coaching, one also needs to take cognisance of the context of the playing environment for the coaches and players in this period in the history of the Silver Ferns. Players were selected because they knew how to play in the style of how we play netball. Their selection was not about the talent being transformed through coaching to play in a different style. There was no requirement for the coach to create representative learning designs; that is, coaching scenarios that reflected aspects of the game that players played through to understand each other's likely responses when such scenarios manifested themselves in actual game situations. Additionally, the amateur teams were only brought together for brief periods of preparation time before international games. There was a social expectation that players could not afford to be away from families or work for extended periods of time. They were first and foremost young women and, secondly, top-class netball players. The limited time to prepare the teams contributed to the pressure on the coach to establish the team and build playing relationships. Team and coaching culture were built around these time constraints, and the coach, and to a lesser extent the captains, had to invent the culture for the team. The coaches, even if they had had a desire to develop a more empowering and inclusive coaching culture, did not have the time to do so; thus they had to be dynamic, autocratic and seen to be in charge. In this sense, they controlled the culture that was achieved through practice and coaching structures.

SECOND ERA (1988–2001)

Coaching within the second period of this study saw a shift in style. The sociocultural landscape of New Zealand had changed dramatically under the Labour government in the 1980s. Greater emphasis was placed upon independent action, taking initiative and being assertive. Also changing were mainstream pedagogical coaching models. Critical thinking about coaching and game playing was becoming more prevalent. In this period in New Zealand two coaching models emerged: Teaching Games for Understanding (TGfU) and athlete-centred coaching. In Australia, a similar change took place and was known as 'game sense'. Both approaches involved player-centred and game-centred learning (GCL) approaches with an emphasis on tactical understanding and individual player responsibility.[118] This changed the style of coaching and method of delivery. It no longer could be command-based, but instead became based on game scenarios that questioned players' understanding of the game. Players were not told what to do, but the coach had to be adept at delivering representative game scenarios for the players to play through. The team culture and playing harmony were delivered through the players experiencing the scenarios together, and in the process learning from each other about how they responded to these situations.

This period also represents the beginning of a professional era in New Zealand sport, and coaches began to reflect this in their broader team structures. Where previously the culture of team stability was achieved by an unshakeable belief in the coach's direction, now players were empowered to contribute to the team and coaching strategy. Players began to inform the team culture in a more holistic way, too, rather than just through their on-court performance.

This style of coaching had mixed fortunes for the winning culture of the Silver Ferns. Initially it was not as successful as measured against the one marker always used to measure the success of the Silver Ferns — matches versus Australia. In the 35 matches between the two countries in this period, the results were lopsided, with 25 wins to Australia and 10 to New Zealand. Crucially, in the ultimate measure of success, matches at the Commonwealth Games and the World Cup were all won by Australia. In the third era, however, the empowerment coaching method would reap benefits. For example, from losing the Commonwealth Games final in 2002 to winning in 2006, of the nine matches played between Australia and New Zealand, the Silver Ferns won seven and lost two — and, crucially, they won the Netball World Cup in 2003. It was felt by the coaches and captains that although previously the empowering approach may not have been successful, it laid the groundwork and coaching expectations for the same approach to be successful in the later years.

MAKING AN EMPOWERING APPROACH WORK

Many words have been written on the empowerment of players through athlete-centred coaching. The approach is often whispered as a given truism of almost Holy Grail status. What is often not said is that for this method to be successful, the team 'mix' has to be right. In terms of player expectations, just as in the previous era, the 'right mix' in this context equates to player expectation of the coaching culture delivered to them. The coach has to be skilled in delivering those expectations in a way that the players accept and embrace. For there to be the right mix, there has to be enough of the players who, besides having a collective will to win and succeed, are sufficiently experienced to capitalise on that empowerment to make it work for the team. The comments from coaches and captains of this era suggest that, as mentioned, initially those qualities were not present, but that the legacy of those early experiences carried over and were the cornerstone of later success.

THIRD ERA (2002–19)

One of the captains who played in this era said she believed that 'there was no perfect coach'. One could add to this by noting that there is no one perfect way to coach, because if there were, then it could be learned and all games would end in a deadlock. Coaches in this later era tended to combine both command-coaching and a degree of empowerment to the players. This pragmatic approach to coaching in a way that was required for the team to do well, based on observations of the players, contexts and opposition, came with an expectation that the coaching would deliver clear directions for the team, using direction that was sometimes delivered quite autocratically. In this sense, regardless of the era, delivering on such direction for the team required the coach to communicate clearly their vision for the team.

A major difference between this era and previous ones was that the Silver Ferns were now full-time or semi-professional players. They came to Silver Ferns camps having already been exposed to high-performance playing and coaching, and to the associated expectations of professional players selected from franchise teams. They were attuned to coaching environments that included assistants, such as attacking and defensive coaches, fitness trainers, medical staff and media consultants. The Silver Ferns now came together not only with this 'baggage' from their professional franchise teams, but also with tremendous knowledge of the game. Silver Ferns coaches now had not only to direct the vision for the team, but also to empower each player to express and contribute her knowledge in order for it to benefit the team.

In summary, the style of coaching within the Silver Ferns in the eras examined has tended to reflect the social and cultural mores of New Zealand society. It has also reflected changes in perceptions of what constitutes good coaching pedagogy. Over this period, there has been a transition from autocratic command styles to a period where a commitment to empowering players was the accepted style. Coaching within the Silver Ferns context leading into the 2020s tends to operate on transparent expectations associated with on- and off-court behaviour, fitness levels, positional leadership, and a commitment to a team plan and vision. The coaching is holistic; it is much more than running, catching and passing drills, and set plays. As a coaching method, it is not confined to a single ideology, but is collaborative, employing pragmatic methods mandated by the requirements of creating a culture within the team that facilitates winning at an elite level of netball.

Emphasis on winning

The emphasis on winning was very inconsistent throughout the three eras, with the interviewees' responses indicating many differing opinions on what winning meant to both captains and coaches. To some, successful performances were measured by the final result, but for others it was more about focusing on the process in order to achieve a consistent winning performance. This misalignment was evident, with many of the coaches interviewed believing that the process and the product displayed on court were the measures of success. In comparison, many of the captains voiced a very strong belief that their purpose was to win in terms of the score, and that losing was never an option.

LEADERSHIP AND WINNING

There were also mixed opinions across the three eras regarding the relationship between leadership and the emphasis placed on winning. Some participants believed that qualities such as leading by example were crucial for leadership to have an influence on winning. Other respondents believed that additional factors beyond leadership could contribute towards winning, including the calibre of players and the potential for injuries to occur. Another common finding was the view that if leadership were to influence winning it had to be in the form of a collective approach, making players feel as if they were a part of a team that could win together.

It was also considered important for such collective leadership to be developed by an effective group of senior players who led by example in order to create a winning culture.

COACHING STYLES AND WINNING

There were variations in the responses from the interviewees regarding the relationship between coaching styles and the emphasis placed on winning. Those from the first era (1960–87) and early in the second era (1988–2001) agreed that there was a strong correlation between effective coaching and winning. A turning point occurred later in the second era as both coaches and captains expressed that winning was considered by them to be a by-product of a coaching style, and winning included many other factors as well as coaching success. Further inconsistencies were found in the final era, with some captains believing the coaching style does have an impact on winning, yet a coach strongly believed it was as much due to the level of ability of her players, not her coaching style.

THE AUSTRALIAN DIAMONDS AND WINNING

Interviewees from the first era identified two main reasons for the Australians having the overall advantage in the trans-Tasman rivalry: they had a greater depth of players to choose from for their national team, and those players were coached to have a winning mentality and a 'killer instinct' — the latter being identified as lacking in New Zealand players. Despite these advantages to Australia, however, the interviewees felt very strongly and believed that New Zealand did extremely well to compete against Australia. Statistics of international matches between Australia and New Zealand between 1960 and 1987 showed that New Zealand recorded 12 wins and Australia 13, indicating that the first era was relatively even between the two.

Australia had a clear winning advantage in the second era, yet the rivalry remained strong, despite the ongoing advantage to Australia in having more players to choose from and a winning mentality. The greater number of high-level competitions in Australia was identified as contributing towards the hardening of players, creating this stronger winning mentality. Further factors identified included the perception of a stronger training ethic and the heightened intensity among Australian players, compared to their New Zealand counterparts (due to greater competition for places on the national team); but again, there remained the strong belief that New Zealand could

The Silver Ferns versus Australia at the 2015 Netball World Cup in Sydney. New Zealand beat Australia 52–47 in the pool stages but lost the final to them 58–55. *Michael Bradley*

match them skill-wise and compete against them. However, the results during this second era indicate otherwise, with New Zealand recording only 10 wins to Australia's 25.

This long-standing rivalry remained evident in the final era (2002–19) and was as strong as in the previous two. Interviewees identified similar factors, namely the Diamonds' mental attitude and toughness and the great depth of players. Many felt that New Zealand had a comparatively poor development plan for feeding players into the national team, and that this lack of depth of strong players forced New Zealand coaches to have to 'make do' with those who were available. But although the Silver Ferns continued to trail the Diamonds in this era, with 32 wins to Australia's 53, they were significantly more competitive in major events, winning two World Championships and two Commonwealth Games.

The consistent pattern of the Silver Ferns losing most of their matches against the Australians, particularly in title-deciding matches, potentially suggests an innate lack of self-belief amongst the players in most periods. It could be said that in order for the Silver Ferns to win, they had to be performing at their very best and Australia below their best. Alongside this is the perception in later eras that the Australians also wanted to win more compared to the Silver Ferns. The significance of the 2019 World Championships victory over Australia is that it reversed this long-term trend. That the Silver Ferns followed up this performance with two wins against Australia in the four-match Constellation Cup series gives fans reason to believe a foundation has been laid for a more equitable era of trans-Tasman competition.

Environmental factors

MEDIA

At first, media influence was very limited, with netball having to fight hard for any coverage. Women were not recognised in sport and the public were not exposed to netball due to this lack of media attention. It was up to the players and coaches during this time to 'educate' reporters on the sport of netball. At the end of the first era, in the 1980s, there was a significant shift as elite netball became one of the four main team sports in New Zealand to receive extensive television coverage.

Throughout the 1990s netball began to receive ever more media coverage as the game moved indoors, making broadcasting a great deal easier. The issue that affected netball most in this second era was that those in Silver Ferns leadership roles needed to be more accessible and responsive to the media. From this time, media demands increased further, with both pre- and post-match interviews with coaches and captains. There was a strong agreement that in order to help netball grow, such increased media demands on the captain and coach were now actively welcomed.

During the third era, the media continued to have a significant impact on the sport and, by extension, on team culture. The media was now an accepted part of the high-performance netball environment. Media training had become a crucial aspect of being a coach and captain of the Silver Ferns, and it was still extremely important to remain on good terms with the media to gain the exposure required for sponsorship and funding purposes. This placed yet another layer of responsibility upon captains and coaches.

Social media also began to influence team culture. It was used as a way to connect to fans, to improve individual reputations, and to help entice sponsors and increase revenue. Although social media provided these opportunities for players, it also exposed them to greater scrutiny, as they could be photographed or recorded at any time. While this meant more exposure for the game, and more money for players, this also placed additional pressure on players to live up to the values of being a Silver Fern '24/7', a non-negotiable part of the team ethos. Therefore, becoming a professional athlete and being able to train full-time does not necessarily mean a sport becomes 'easier' for players, because a different set of pressures is also created.

PREGNANCY

Historically, netball is one of the few team sports that have been played, administered and coached by women, for women, so female leadership is the norm in the game. Interviewees acknowledged that pregnancy influenced the team culture, but not in a negative way; the impact of pregnant players, or players returning after giving birth, seemed to be around how to address these pregnancies and provide support.

In the first era, netball was mostly played by unmarried or childless women. Pregnancy became much more of an issue in the second era. Some players who became pregnant felt the strain of a perceived lack of support from the coach and from Netball New Zealand, relating to mental and emotional capacity, and also financial demands. This perceived lack of support seemed still to be strongly evident throughout the second and even third eras, and some interviewees clearly found it very hard to juggle motherhood with an elite netball playing career.

Recently, it has become more common for players who become pregnant to return to netball after giving birth, and the findings did indicate a growing level of support for them as an evolving part of Silver Ferns culture. Indeed, another important finding showed that motherhood is increasingly accepted in the female sporting career, with some believing that returning to international sport after having children is an empowering action and an implicit statement on what women can do. Despite this, it is also believed that coaches and Netball New Zealand need to be better prepared for this to happen and accept it as part of high-performance female sport.

Implications for coaches from the research

To what extent are the findings of this research, which has been conducted on an international team, relevant for coaches at regional, age-group and, indeed, community-level netball? Although it is acknowledged that high-performance and community sport operate in very different contexts, there are some general observations which might be made.

TEAM CULTURE

- The creation and development of team culture is extremely important. While the development of team values, such as work ethic, can be useful towards creating a team culture, they do not necessarily need to be done formally, nor indeed be explicit.
- Symbols can play an important part in the culture of a team, but it is important to recognise that such symbols may differ between teams and eras. For example, some symbols may be initiated by players, and therefore a change in players in the team may be a timely opportunity to change a team's symbols.
- There is generally a positive correlation between good team culture and winning. Nonetheless, coaches should consider whether it is worthwhile focusing on creating a good culture irrespective of results. The argument for doing so is that it provides a better experience for players, who accordingly are more likely to remain involved in the game, which might be regarded as being as important as the results.
- The embracing and acceptance of various cultures — for example, through sharing different cultural rites and rituals, such as a waiata — does not refer purely to ethnicities, but rather may involve the acceptance of players and the different personalities and skills they bring to the team.

Many coaches do not have the background, tools or knowledge required for developing team culture. Therefore, national sporting organisations such as Netball New Zealand need to consider the importance of developing and offering modules on developing team culture both for elite and community-based coaches, and to provide coaches with an understanding of how to enhance this aspect of team development.

LEADERSHIP

- Coaches should keep an open mind on what leadership may look like in their team at the beginning of the season.
- Having one captain in sole charge of a team may not always produce effective leadership, as they quite often need to be supported by other senior players.
- Leadership groups can be very effective, particularly when they include younger team members and not just seniors.
- Players who lead by example via their performance, work ethic and informal values are usually viewed by the team as being the best leaders.
- In some teams where there is a clear, natural leader who commands the respect of the whole team, it may work best if they are placed in sole charge of the team.
- Developing effective leadership groups takes time and may not be achieved over the duration of one season, but rather may take multiple seasons.
- Coaches may need to use a blend of styles. It can be effective to combine the empowering approach with the command/autocratic approach, as not all players prefer or respond well to one particular coaching style. Successful coaches find that there is a time and place for each approach, and understand what works best for their team. This will largely depend on the players.

EMPHASIS ON WINNING

- In order to create a 'winning' team culture, it is vital to establish what this term means to everyone in the team, both players and management. Some may view winning in terms of the final score or result, while others may consider it as being the product of the performance the team puts out on court.
- What it means to win may differ significantly for teams at various levels, from high school to representative or national level; nonetheless, in order to succeed in either aspect of winning — that is, results or performance — the whole team must be in agreement.

Action between Waitākere 1 and Eastern BOP during the Netball New Zealand Under 17 Champs at Waitākere, Auckland, in 2019.
Michael Bradley

Major event statistics

World Cups

YEAR	RESULT	VS AUSTRALIA
1963	2nd vs Australia (round-robin)	L 36–37
1967	1st vs Australia (round-robin)	W 40–34
1971	2nd vs Australia (round-robin)	L 42–48
1975	3rd vs Trinidad & Tobago (round-robin)	D 34–34
1979	1st equal Australia/Trinidad & Tobago (round-robin)	L 36–38
1983	2nd vs Australia (round-robin)	L 42–47
1987	1st vs Australia (round-robin)	W 39–28
1991	2nd vs Australia	L 52–53
1995	3rd vs England	L 44–45
1999	2nd vs Australia	L 41–42
2003	1st vs Australia	W 49–47
2007	2nd vs Australia	L 38–42
2011	2nd vs Australia	L 57–58
2015	2nd vs Australia	L 55–58
2019	1st vs Australia	W 52–51

World Games

YEAR	RESULT	VS AUSTRALIA
1985	1st vs Australia	W 39–37
1989	1st vs Australia	W 33–29
1993	2nd vs Australia	L 36–62

Source: www.mynetball.co.nz

Commonwealth Games

YEAR	RESULT	VS AUSTRALIA
1998	2nd vs Australia	L 39–42
2002	2nd vs Australia	L 55–57
2006	1st vs Australia	W 60–55
2010	1st vs Australia	W 66–64
2014	2nd vs Australia	L 40–58
2018	4th place	L 44–65

Fast5 World Series

YEAR	RESULT
2009	1st vs Jamaica
2010	1st vs England
2011	2nd vs England
2012	1st vs England
2013	1st vs Australia
2014	1st vs Australia
2015	Not played
2016	1st vs Australia
2017	4th place
2018	1st vs Jamaica
2019	Not played

Source: www.mynetball.co.nz

Notes

1 Television New Zealand, '"Australians think they walk on water" — Dame Lois Muir speaks about Silver Ferns' victory, watching match from bed', https://www.tvnz.co.nz/one-news/sport/netball/australians-think-they-walk-water-dame-lois-muir-speaks-silver-ferns-victory-watching-match-bed, accessed 20 December 2019.

2 https://www.youtube.com/watch?v=4V8bMfWmxSI

3 Ibid.

4 For a more detailed discussion of these themes, see Farah Palmer, 'Winning Black Ferns', in Tom Johnson, Andy Martin and Geoff Watson (eds), *Legends in Black: New Zealand Rugby Greats on Why We Win* (Auckland: Penguin, 2014), pp. 260–83, and 'Stories of Haka and Women's Rugby in Aotearoa New Zealand: Weaving Identities and Ideologies Together', *International Journal of the History of Sport* 33, no. 17 (2016): 2169–84.

5 Netball New Zealand, 'Coaches — Taini Jamison', https://www.silverferns.co.nz/silver-ferns/history/coaches/taini-jamison.html, accessed 22 November 2019.

6 We are grateful to Ian Culpan for information on Sam Lewis. Ian Culpan and Bob Stothart, 'Lewis, Sam', in R. A. Stothart with Ian Culpan, *For the Record: An Encyclopaedia of Historical Aspects of New Zealand Physical Education* (Christchurch: School of Sciences and Physical Education, University of Canterbury, 2012).

7 Netball New Zealand, 'Lois Muir', https://www.silverferns.co.nz/silver-ferns/history/coaches/lois-muir.html, accessed 22 November 2019.

8 Ibid.

9 Netball New Zealand, 'Coaches — Lyn Gunson', https://www.silverferns.co.nz/silver-ferns/history/coaches/lyn-gunson.html, accessed 22 November 2019.

10 Ibid.

11 Netball New Zealand, 'Coaches — Leigh Gibbs', https://www.silverferns.co.nz/silver-ferns/history/coaches/leigh-gibbs.html, accessed 22 November 2019.

12 'Lesley Rumball', https://en.wikipedia.org/wiki/Lesley_Rumball, accessed 22 November 2019; Netball New Zealand, 'Players — Lesley Rumball (nee Nicol)', https://www.silverferns.co.nz/silver-ferns/history/players/lesley-rumball.html, accessed 22 November 2019.

13 'Bernice Mene', https://en.wikipedia.org/wiki/Bernice_Mene; Netball New Zealand, 'Players — Bernice Mene', https://www.silverferns.co.nz/silver-ferns/history/players/bernice-mene.html, both accessed 22 November 2019.

14 Netball New Zealand, 'Coaches — Ruth Aitken', https://www.silverferns.co.nz/silver-ferns/history/coaches/ruth-aitken.html, accessed 22 November 2019.

15 Ibid.

16 'Ruth Aitken', https://en.wikipedia.org/wiki/Ruth_Aitken; Singapore Netball, 'National Coach Ruth Aitken to Step Down after 2016 Season', https://www.netball.org.sg/News/Latest-News/netball-national-coach-Ruth-Aitken-to-step-down-after-2016-season, both accessed 22 November 2019.

17 Netball New Zealand, 'Players — Julie Seymour (nee Dawson)', https://www.silverferns.co.nz/silver-ferns/history/players/julie-seymour.html, accessed 22 November 2019.

18 Netball New Zealand, 'Casey Kopua (nee Williams)', https://www.silverferns.co.nz/silver-ferns/history/players/casey-kopua.html, accessed 22 November 2019; 'Casey Kopua', https://en.wikipedia.org/wiki/Casey_Kopua.

19 https://www.youtube.com/watch?v=uDwyW2uPBgI

20 https://www.tvnz.co.nz/one-news/sport/netball/p-u-r-e-mantra-driving-silver-ferns-netball-world-cup

21 https://www.newsroom.co.nz/2019/07/22/692909/this-world-cups-for-you-casey-kopua#

22 Kevin Norquay, 'Netball World Cup: Silver Ferns are sadly undervalued and underpaid', *Stuff*, 22 July 2019, https://www.stuff.co.nz/sport/opinion/114425694/netball-world-cup-silver-ferns-are-undervalued-and-underpaid-and-here-are-the-numbers-to-prove-it, accessed 9 August 2019.

23 Peter Hawes and Lizzy Barker, *Court in the Spotlight: History of New Zealand Netball* (Christchurch: Netball New Zealand, 1999), p. 142.

24 Richard Holt, *Sport and the British: A Modern History* (Oxford: Clarendon, 1989), pp. 74–86, 118–34.

25 Kathleen McCrone, *Sport and the Physical Emancipation of English Women* (London: Routledge, 1988); Jennifer Hargreaves, *Sporting Females: Critical Issues in the History and Sociology of Women's Sports* (London: Routledge, 1994); Holt, *Sport and the British*, pp. 74–134.

26 Keith Myerscough, 'The Game with No Name: The Invention of Basketball', *International Journal of the History of Sport* 12, no. 1 (1995): 137–52, cited in Geoff Andrew, '"A Girl's Game — And a Good One Too": A Critical Analysis of New Zealand Netball', unpublished master's thesis, University of Canterbury, 1997, p. 20.

27 Sheila Fletcher, 'The Making and Breaking of a Female Tradition: Women's Physical Education in Britain, 1880–1980', *International Journal of the History of Sport* 2, no. 1 (1985): 32.

28 Hargreaves, *Sporting Females,* pp. 74–87, 124.

29 Ian Jobling and Pamela Barham, 'The Development of Netball and the All-Australia Women's Basketball Association (AAWBBA): 1891–1939', *Sporting Traditions* 8, no. 1 (1991): 29–31. Hawes and Barker, *Court in the Spotlight,* pp. 12–13.

30 Hawes and Barker, *Court in the Spotlight,* p. 70.

31 Greg Ryan and Geoff Watson, *Sport and the New Zealanders: A History* (Auckland: Auckland University Press, 2018), pp. 54–144; Len Richardson, 'Parties and Political Change', in G. W. Rice (ed.), *The Oxford History of New Zealand* (Auckland: Oxford University Press, 1992), vol. 2, pp. 201–14.

32 Catherine Smith, 'Control of the Female Body: Physical Training at Three New Zealand Girls' High Schools 1880s–1920s', *Sporting Traditions* 13, no. 2 (1997): 59–71.

33 Ibid., p. 60.

34 Ryan and Watson, *Sport and the New Zealanders*, pp. 100–10.

35 Jennifer Curtin, 'Before the "Black Ferns": Tracing the Development of Women's Rugby in New Zealand', *International Journal of the History of Sport* 33, no. 17 (2016): 2075–78.

36 Barbara Cox, 'The Rise and Fall of "The Girl Footballer" in New Zealand during 1921', *International Journal of the History of Sport* 29, no. 3 (2012): 444–71.

37 *Star,* 12 August 1896, p. 2.

38 *Wanganui Herald,* 19 December 1898, p. 2; *Wanganui Chronicle,* 19 December 1899, p. 2; *Wanganui Chronicle,* 18 December 1900, p. 2.

39 John Nauright, 'Netball and the Creation of a Female Sporting Culture in New Zealand', *Journal of Physical Education New Zealand* 29, no. 2 (1996): 14; *Evening Star,* 27 October 1900, p. 2.

40 M. A. E. Hammer, '"Something Else in the World to Live For": Sport and the Physical Emancipation of Women and Girls in Auckland 1880–1920', unpublished master's thesis, University of Auckland, 1990, p. 48.

41 Ibid.

42 Sandra Coney, *Every Girl: A History of Women and the YWCA in Auckland 1885–1985* (Auckland: Auckland YWCA, 1986), pp. 170, 171–81.

43 Ryan and Watson, *Sport and the New Zealanders,* pp. 151–56.

44 Andrew, '"A Girl's Game — And a Good One Too"', pp. 37, 56.

45 Ibid., pp. 47–77; Hawes and Barker, *Court in the Spotlight,* pp. 17–34.

46 Ruth Fry, '"Don't Let Down the Side": Physical Education in the Curriculum for New Zealand Schoolgirls 1900–1945', in Barbara Brookes, Charlotte Macdonald and Margaret Tennant (eds), *Women in History: Essays on European Women in New Zealand* (Wellington: Allen & Unwin, 1986), pp. 109–11.

47 Andrew, '"A Girl's Game — And a Good One Too"', p. 140.

48 Geoff Watson, 'An Age of Expansion: The Widening Sporting World in Palmerston North and New Zealand', in Rachael Bell (ed.), *New Zealand Between the Wars* (Auckland: Massey University Press, 2017), pp. 320–21, 326.

49 Report of Inspector of Native Schools, 'Education of Native Children', *Appendices to the Journal of the House of Representatives* (AJHR), 1932, E-3, 4.

50 Ryan and Watson, *Sport and the New Zealanders*, p. 162.

51 Dana Johannsen, 'New Zealand's First Captain Led Her Team on a Special Journey', in Mike Bynum (ed.), *Greatest Moments in New Zealand Netball History* (Chicago: Canada Hockey LLC, 2011), pp. 116–17.

52 John Nauright, 'Netball, Media Representation of Women and the Crisis of Male Hegemony in New Zealand', in John Nauright (ed.), *Sport, Power and Society in New Zealand: Historical and Contemporary Perspectives* (Australian Society for Sports History: *ASSH Studies in Sports History*, no. 11, 1999), pp. 50–57.

53 Hawes and Barker, *Court in the Spotlight*, p. 27.

54 Ibid., pp. 23–24, 16.

55 *Otago Daily Times*, 8 April 1926, p. 6, cited in Nauright, 'Netball, Media Representation of Women', p. 52.

56 Nauright, 'Netball and the Creation of a Female Sporting Culture in New Zealand', p. 15.

57 Jobling and Barham, 'The Development of Netball', pp. 39–44. Hawes and Barker, *Court in the Spotlight*, p. 34.

58 Ryan and Watson, *Sport and the New Zealanders*, pp. 153–54, 169–72.

59 Ibid., pp. 199–205.

60 Andrew, '"A Girl's Game — And a Good One Too"', pp. 56–57; Netball New Zealand, 'History', http://www.netballnz.co.nz/our-game/history/1960-1990, accessed 31 May 2019.

61 Hawes and Barker, *Court in the Spotlight*, pp. 43–48.

62 Ibid., pp. 47–50.

63 Ibid., pp. 49–52.

64 Ibid., p. 65.

65 Hawes and Barker, *Court in the Spotlight*, pp. 53–70; Lana McCarthy, 'Coaches, Captains and Cultural Constructs: A Case Study of the Silver Ferns', unpublished doctoral thesis, Massey University, Palmerston North, 2019, p. 293.

66 Hawes and Barker, *Court in the Spotlight*, pp. 69–75.

67 Netball New Zealand, 'History 1960–1990', http://www.netballnz.co.nz/our-game/history/1960–1990, accessed 19 June 2019.

68 Hawes and Barker, *Court in the Spotlight,* p. 77; Bill Keane, '"Ex-pats" and "Poofters" Rebuild the Nation: 1982, Kiwi Culture and the All Whites on the Road to Spain', in Brad Patterson (ed.), *Sport, Society and Culture in New Zealand* (Wellington: Stout Research Centre, 1999), pp. 56–60.

69 McCarthy, 'Coaches, Captains, and Cultural Constructs', pp. 119–20.

70 Dorothy Simons, *New Zealand's Champion Sportswomen* (Auckland: Moa, 1982), pp. 145–46.

71 Hawes and Barker, *Court in the Spotlight,* pp. 69, 77; McCarthy, 'Coaches, Captains and Cultural Constructs', p. 121.

72 Marian Smith and Brian Humberstone, *Netball: The Greatest Team Sport for Women* (Auckland: Cassell, 1978), pp. 87–89.

73 McCarthy, 'Coaches, Captains and Cultural Constructs', p. 122; Barbara Brookes, *A History of New Zealand Women* (Wellington: Bridget Williams, 2016), 337–77.

74 Linda Jones and John Costello, *The Linda Jones Story* (Auckland: Moa, 1979.

75 Andrew, '"A Girl's Game — And a Good One Too"', pp. 78–81.

76 Hawes and Barker, *Court in the Spotlight,* pp. 99–105.

77 Andrew, '"A Girl's Game — And a Good One Too"', p. 125.

78 Nauright, 'Netball, Media Representation of Women', pp. 58–60; John Nauright and Jayne Broomhall, 'A Woman's Game: The Development of Netball and a Female Sporting Culture in New Zealand 1906–70', *International Journal of the History of Sport* 11, no. 3 (1994): 401–03.

79 McCarthy, 'Coaches, Captains and Cultural Constructs', p. 120.

80 Ibid., p. 124.

81 Lois Muir and Joseph Romanos, *Lois Muir on Netball* (Auckland: Reed Methuen, 1985); Simons, *New Zealand's Champion Sportswomen,* pp. 138–56; Joseph Romanos, *Makers of Champions: Great NZ Coaches* (Lower Hutt: Mills, 1986), pp. 123–39.

82 Lois Muir, *Netball: A Guide for Teachers, Coaches and Players* (Wellington: Government Printer, 1989), pp. 39–40; Andrew, '"A Girl's Game — And a Good One Too"', p. 60.

83 Adrienne Simpson, 'New Zealand's Wicket Women', in Patterson, *Sport, Society and Culture*, p. 71.

84 Ryan and Watson, *Sport and the New Zealanders,* pp. 294–301; Sarah Beaman, *Women and Cricket: Cricket and Women* (Auckland, Lincoln: New Zealand Cricket, 2016), pp.12–13.

85 For example, in 1993–94, 38 per cent of New Zealand Cricket's governance structure was female; in 2016 it was 6.4 per cent. Beaman, *Women and Cricket*, p. 14.

86 Suzanne McFadden, 'Netball', Te Ara — the Encyclopedia of New Zealand,

http://www.TeAra.govt.nz/en/netball, accessed 21 November 2019.

87 Hawes and Barker, *Court in the Spotlight,* pp. 142–45.

88 Andrew, '"A Girl's Game — And a Good One Too"', pp. 70–73.

89 Television New Zealand, 'High Performing NZ Men's Netball Team Draws More Boys to Sport', https://www.tvnz.co.nz/one-news/sport/netball/high-performing-nz-mens-netball-team-draws-more-boys-sport, accessed 21 November 2019.

90 Hawes and Barker, *Court in the Spotlight,* pp. 167–68, 183–85.

91 Ian Dougherty, *Southern Sting: The Team that Inspired a Region* (Auckland: Exisle, 2004), p. 24; Adine Wilson, *Adine Wilson: Skills and Performance* (Auckland: Hodder Moa, 2008), p. 61; Joseph Romanos, *The Judas Game* (Wellington: Darius, 2002), p. 23.

92 Wilson, *Adine Wilson,* pp. 60–61.

93 McCarthy, 'Coaches, Captains and Cultural Constructs', p. 131.

94 Hawes and Barker, *Court in the Spotlight,* pp. 196–97; Netball New Zealand, 'History', http://www.netballnz.co.nz/our-game/history/1990–1999, accessed 31 May 2019.

95 Hawes and Barker, *Court in the Spotlight,* pp. 196–97.

96 Dana Johannsen, 'Netball's Long Road to Equality', *New Zealand Herald,* 19 September 2008. In Australia the ANZ Championship replaced the Commonwealth Bank Trophy.

97 Dana Johannsen, 'Anatomy of a Split', *New Zealand Herald,* 14 May 2016.

98 Cheree Kinnear, 'Was New Zealand's Split from the Former Trans-Tasman Championship a Mistake?', *New Zealand Herald,* 13 August 2018.

99 Lana McCarthy, 'Coaches, Captains and Cultural Constructs', p. 139.

100 Brendon Egan, 'Leading Silver Ferns Earn a 10th of Salary of Millionaire All Black Kieran Read', *Stuff,* 3 January 2018; https://www.stuff.co.nz/sport/netball/100028462/semiprofessional-pay-for-professional-play-thats-the-life-of-a-netballer, accessed 31 May 2019.

101 Australian Associated Press, 'World Cup–Winning NZ Netballers Rewarded with Unprecedented Payment after Outcry', cited in *The Guardian,* 25 July 2019, https://www.theguardian.com/sport/2019/jul/25/world-cup-winning-nz-netballers-rewarded-with-unprecedented-payment-after-outcry, accessed 30 August 2019.

102 Liam Napier, 'Wages Less than Fern-tastic for NZ Netballers', *Stuff,* 11 August 2013, http://www.stuff.co.nz/sport/9027470/Wages-less-than-Fern-tastic-for-NZ-netballers, accessed 31 May 2019.

103 McCarthy, 'Coaches, Captains and Cultural Constructs', p. 143.

104 Dana Johannsen, 'Netball's Long Road to Equality', *New Zealand Herald,* 19 September, 2008.

105 Hockey New Zealand, *Summary of Review Findings,* 25 February 2019, pp. 1–2; Philippa Muir, *Independent Review into NZ Football: Public*

Recommendations and Findings (Auckland: Simpson Grierson, 3 October 2018), pp. 8–13.

106 Netball New Zealand, *Ninety-Fourth Annual Report 2018*, p. 12.

107 Netball New Zealand, 'History', http://www.netballnz.co.nz/our-game/history/2010-now; Netball New Zealand, 'Partners', http://www.netballnz.co.nz/about/partners, accessed 31 May 2019.

108 McCarthy, 'Coaches, Captains and Cultural Constructs', pp. 131–32, 143–44.

109 Olivia Caldwell, 'Elite Athlete or Elite Mum', *Sunday Star-Times*, 8 July 2018, p. A8; Liam Napier, 'Baby on Board', *Sunday Star-Times*, 8 May 2016, p. B3.

110 McCarthy, 'Coaches, Captains and Cultural Constructs', p. 144.

111 Netball New Zealand, 'History', http://www.netballnz.co.nz/our-game/history/2000–2009, accessed 31 May 2019.

112 Netball New Zealand, 'History', http://www.netballnz.co.nz/our-game/history/2010-now, accessed 31 May 2019.

113 Netball New Zealand, *2018 Commonwealth Games Review* (Auckland: Netball New Zealand, 2018), pp. 1–4.

114 Edgar Schein, *Organizational Culture and Leadership* (San Francisco: Jossey-Bass, 2010).

115 For a more detailed analysis of the findings discussed in this chapter see McCarthy, 'Coaches, Captains and Cultural Constructs'.

116 Tom Johnson, 'Winning Ways', in Tom Johnson, Andy Martin, Geoff Watson and Margot Butcher (eds), *Legends in Black: New Zealand Rugby Greats on Why We Win* (Auckland: Penguin, 2014), p. 230.

117 Dennis Slade, Andy Martin and Geoff Watson, 'The Evolving Development of Teaching and Coaching Games and Sports in New Zealand', *Physical Education New Zealand* 52, no. 2 (2018): 4–27.

118 Slade, Martin and Watson, 'The Evolving Development', pp. 17–18.

About the contributors

Dr Lana McCarthy is a lecturer in teacher education at Charles Sturt University. She completed her doctoral thesis, 'Coaches, Captains and Constructing Culture: A Case Study of the Silver Ferns', at Massey University in 2019. Lana has a background as a physical education and health teacher at Freyberg High School, a netball development officer at Netball Manawatū, a regional sport advisor at Sport Manawatū, and a senior tutor and assistant lecturer in physical education at Massey University. Lana's netball-playing career began as a young primary school student in Upper Hutt and then Masterton. She progressed throughout the Wairarapa representative teams, and was named in the Wellington Regional Talent Identification Squad in her final year of high school. The move to Palmerston North for university allowed her to play for the Manawatū Under 19 representative team and she has been a member of the Feilding A1 Club netball team for the past decade, playing in the Manawatū Premier 1 competition. During this time her attention turned to coaching and she is now a high-performance netball coach. Recently she has coached the Palmerston North Girls' High School Senior A1, the Manawatū Under 19 and Under 17 representative teams and the Central Zone Under 23 netball team, and she was selected for the 'Pathway to Pulse' high-performance programme.

Dr Andrew John Martin is a professor of sport management and physical education in the School of Sport, Exercise and Nutrition, Massey University. His research focus is on sport-related experiential learning settings and he has undertaken a number of studies on Outward Bound, including his PhD. In 2014 he was co-author of *Legends in Black*, a bestselling book about why the All Blacks win. Andrew has followed Lana's postgraduate study with keen interest, supervising both her master's and doctoral thesis. His own career began in the United Kingdom teaching mathematics and coaching football at Millfield, a top public school. Following on from his master's degree at Loughborough University, he managed programmes and events for a leading health-club facility near London. After moving to New Zealand in 1993 he worked as event manager for the Hillary Commission Big Coast series of mountain bike treks. In 1994 he took up his current position at Massey University and now manages a successful series of children's triathlon events in Manawatū. He has participated in the New Zealand Ironman and most recently for New Zealand at the age-group World Triathlon Championships. He holds professional coaching qualifications in football and tennis, and has been actively involved in coaching at both junior and senior level.

Dr Geoff Watson is an associate professor in the School of Humanities, Massey University. His research focus is sports history. He is the principal author of *Seasons of Honour: A Centennial History of New Zealand Hockey 1902–2002* (2002) and *Sporting Foundations of New Zealand Indians: A Fifty-year History of the New Zealand Indian Sports Association* (2012). He is co-author of *Sport and the New Zealanders: A History* (2018), *Sport Development in Action: Plan, Programme, Practice* (2019) and *Legends in Black: New Zealand Rugby Greats on Why We Win* (2014). He teaches a paper in sports history at Massey University and was also one of Lana's supervisors for her doctoral thesis. He takes an interest in most sports and has been extensively involved at grass-roots level, including coaching Massey University hockey teams and participating in long-distance running.

Dr Dennis Slade is an associate professor in the School of Sport, Exercise and Nutrition at Massey University. With an extensive background in secondary school physical education, Dennis has also worked in the higher education sector since 1990, delivering undergraduate courses in pre-service teacher education, sport pedagogy and coaching. A member of the international Teaching Games for Understanding (TGfU) task force, Dennis has an extensive record of producing texts, multimedia resources and publishing research on game-centred learning. Internationally and nationally he has delivered masterclasses on TGfU and provided extensive multidisciplinary programmes and workshops for teachers and coaches at both grass-roots and elite levels of sport. Dennis has played sport at an international level, coaching national league hockey and as the head coach of the New Zealand Under 16 boys' hockey team. Dennis was also one of Lana's PhD supervisors and a discipline leader in physical education at Massey University.

Acknowledgements

The authors would like to thank all the Silver Ferns players, captains and coaches who have participated in interviews for this work. Your insights and passion for the Silver Ferns have been humbling. They also acknowledge the support of Netball New Zealand, particularly their assistance in sourcing illustrations.

The authors gratefully acknowledge the expertise and support of Nicola Legat, Tracey Borgfeldt and Anna Bowbyes at Massey University Press in bringing this book to publication.

This book would also not have come together without the support of our families — thank you to all, and a big thank you to Levinia Paku for transcribing the interviews.

Index

Page numbers in **bold** refer to images

MASSEY
UNIVERSITY
PRESS

First published in 2020 by Massey University Press
Private Bag 102904, North Shore Mail Centre
Auckland 0745, New Zealand
www.masseypress.ac.nz

Design by Sarah Elworthy
Front cover image Marty Melville/Photosport: Silver Ferns Jane Watson and Katrina Rore and Australian Diamonds Gretel Tippett and Caitlin Bassett compete for the ball during a Constellation Cup netball match in Wellington in 2018. Back cover image Netball New Zealand: The New Zealand netball team perform a haka at the first World Tournament, held in England in 1963.

A catalogue record for this book is available from the National Library of New Zealand

Printed and bound in New Zealand by Printlink

ISBN: 978-0-9951135-5-8